THE LOOK AND LEARN BOOK 1974

CONTENTS	PAGE

D0269589

STRANGE CREATURES FROM THE EAST

Some of the strangest looking creatures of the animal kingdom are found in the East. Curiosities like the proboscis monkey shown in the picture below, have features which make them look quite ridiculous. This monkey's snout, for example, looks like the hooked beak of some huge bird of prey. But it is these odd characteristics which help many animals to survive in the world.

This spectacular-looking creature is called the Japanese rooster, a descendant of the jungle fowl, which is specially bred for exhibition purposes. The incredibly long tail grows at the rate of three feet each year until it reaches a remarkable length of 20 feet! The bird cannot run about, but has to stay on its perch in case its wonderful tail gets tangled up.

The taguans or Indian flying squirrels are graceful creatures that can cover a distance of sixty to eighty yards in one magnificent leap, using their tails as rudders. They inhabit the forests of India and dine on nuts and fruit.

The kissing gourami fish which are found in the freshwater pools of South East Asia have wide, protruding lips which they use as suckers for feeding. Apart from this unusual feature, the gourami are equipped with special breathing apparatus in a cavity above each gill which enables them to breathe in water which contains no oxygen.

With its four webbed feet supporting its light weight, the flying frog of Borneo can make a gliding descent of 40 feet like a parachutist.

Another excellent 'parachutist' is the flying Gecko of South East Asia which can leap into the air to avoid an attacking predator.

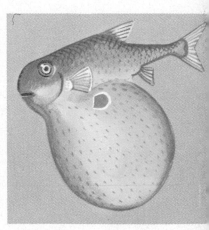

When the poisonous puffer fish is taken out of water it swells up like a gigantic balloon by gulping great quantities of air.

When the sac fish detects danger it will blow up its stomach into a huge balloon to frighten its enemy away.

This ugly animal of Asia is the tube-nosed fruit bat, so-called because of the tubes on its face and its fondness for eating fruit.

This curious-looking creature with its large snout which gives its head an elephant-like appearance, is the Malayan tapir. An excellent swimmer, the tapir seeks safety from enemies by making for the nearest pool.

BIRDS IN LEGEND

For centuries birds have fired the imagination of Man and have been the subject of some of the most remarkable stories ever told.

SUPREME among the supernatural beings worshipped by the Red Indian tribes of North America was the gigantic, terrifying Thunder Bird.

Soaring through the skies like a ferocious monster, with eyes which flashed lightning and beating wings which rolled thunder, this magnificent creature struck terror into the hearts of the men and women who lived along the coasts at the North West Pacific.

And not without cause. For the Thunder Bird was believed to feed on bison and carry off fully grown men with one spectacular sweep of its massive wing.

But to the Red Indians the Thunder Bird was also a sacred spirit and a kindly god, for it was he who prevented the earth from drying up and vegetation from dying.

Birds like the Thunder Bird, which were considered to be divine spirits, appear in all the religions and mythologies of ancient peoples and played a very important part in their lives.

The Eagle, for example, has been a symbol of war and fertility since 3000 B.C. and even before that date, it played an important part in the magic and religion which were so powerful an influence on primitive peoples.

Later, the powers exercised by these birds and animals became greater and greater until people began to worship them as gods. And so these creatures passed into the wonderful myths and legends of peoples all over the world.

The very earliest gods of ancient

It was only in quite recent times that scientists discovered evidence that the legend of the Thunder Bird may have been based on fact. The discovery of the remains of a prehistoric bird which resembled an eagle but had a skull twice the size of that of the largest living eagles revealed that birds of prey much larger than any known today once inhabited Indian territory. It was probably from tales about the attacks of these birds on human beings that the legend of the terrifying Thunder Bird began.

The terrifying Thunder Bird

The Chough

The fabulous Phoenix

The Stork

A Raven at the Tower

Like the hawk and the falcon, the Ibis was held sacred by the ancient Egyptians because they believed that their god Thoth once disguised himself as this bird.

Egypt were all represented as birds and animals. The Egyptians believed that these divine creatures led them into battle, and even fought for them.

Gradually these animal deities, or gods, began to take human form and this is why so many of the gods worshipped by ancient races have the heads of birds and animals.

The falcon was considered pre-eminent among divine beings from the earliest times and so the Egyptian sky god, Thoth, was often portrayed as a falcon in the statues which adorned his temples.

The hawk, too, was held sacred by the Egyptians because it was the form assumed by Ra, the creator and ruler of the world; the all-powerful sun god.

Superstition towards these sacred creatures was so deeply rooted in the minds of all Egyptians that to kill one of them was considered the very worst crime that a man could commit. Even if one of these birds was killed by accident the "murderer" was instantly put to death.

Perhaps the most famous of all mythical creatures is the Phoenix, the fabulous Eagle-like bird of Arabia with its magnificently-coloured plumage, who, according to different versions of the legend, lived from 250 to 7,000 years.

Most people believe that it lives for 500 years, after which time it travels to Egypt and there "buries itself in a nest of spices in which,

being set on fire by the sun or some other secret power, it burns itself and out of its ashes rises another."

It is for this mystical magical act of arising from the ashes of its dead self to be reborn that the Phoenix is most famous. Its name has even passed into our language as a symbol of rebirth.

The albatross is another fabled bird that is steeped in legend. It appears in almost every exciting tale of the sea perhaps because of its habit of following ships for hundreds of miles, and because it is often the only living creature seen for days in the southern seas.

For a long time sailors believed that if they killed an albatross a great disaster would befall them. In Samuel Taylor Coleridge's famous poem, *The Rime of the Ancient Mariner*, a sailor shoots an albatross and brings a curse upon the ship.

Even today some birds are still held sacred because the legends attached to them have been passed on from one century to another. The stork is held sacred in Sweden because there is a legend that it flew round the cross while Jesus Christ was being crucified crying "Shyrka, Shyrka" which means "Strengthen, strengthen."

In Cornwall the chough is protected because the soul of King Arthur is fabled to have migrated into one of these birds and the chough is, therefore, considered a reincarnation of the legendary king.

At the Tower of London the ravens are carefully guarded and their wings have been clipped to stop them from flying away because of the famous legend that if the Tower loses its ravens disaster will befall the land.

The Roman Eagles, the images which the legions used as emblems, were also considered sacred and soldiers would face any danger, often to the point of risking their lives, rather than allow one to be captured.

Following the Roman example, Napoleon I displayed the eagle on the standards of his regiments, and for years his "French Eagles" were the invincible soldiers of Europe.

So great was the powerful symbol of the Eagle that it has still retained its importance and many countries today use the eagle as a national emblem.

In the United States of America the President's Standard displays the American Eagle and in Austria the State Flag bears the portrait of a black eagle grasping a hammer and sickle in its talons.

We can only wonder at such a creature which has been held sacred by so many people of different races and creeds for over 5,000 years.

But with man's unique ability to exaggerate with every telling of a tale, perhaps it is not so surprising that the eagle and many other birds are still the subject of countless fantastic stories.

Napoleonic Eagle

It is not surprising that the magnificent eagle has appeared in so many myths and legends told by men all over the world.

The sight of this splendid king of birds with its powerful, majestic flight, and supreme dignity could fire the weakest imagination and inspire men to tell wonderful tales of its terrifying power.

For centuries this bird has been a symbol of war and nobility. The Golden Eagle and the Spread Eagle were the heraldic emblems of the eastern emperors and were the ensigns of the ancient kings of Babylon and Persia.

There have always been legends that eagles carry off children and devour them. Many people really believed these fables and some of the old inns of England were actually called 'The Eagle and The Child'.

There is hardly any truth in such tales, although it is easy to see why they were believed when we consider that an eagle can seize a fawn which is as heavy as a baby.

Austrian Eagle

U.S.A. Eagle

7

Dinosaurs dominated the world for 200 million years. Then, suddenly, they were obliterated from the face of the earth. What was it that had destroyed the most awesome animals ever generated by the fruitful earth?

WHY DID THEY VANISH?

PRIMITIVE MAMMAL FOSSILS NO DINOSAUR BONES

BARREN

ROCK

NUMEROUS DINOSAUR FOSSIL

The narrow black line mar the break between the age of reptiles and the age of mammals.

O F all the mysteries that have intrigued students of palaeontology, none is more tantalizing than the mass extinction of the great dinosaurs and their kin.

In spite of the yearly account of some prehistoric monster, resembling a plesiosaur, seen in Loch Ness, it is an unquestionable fact that the last dinosaur perished around seventy million years ago at the close of the Cretaceous Period, long before the

first primate—let alone Man—had seen the strange and fearful world of the great reptiles, or had a chance to tremble before the thunder of Ceratopsian herds pounding across the plains.

Since the beginning of life, extinction has been the rule, rather than the exception.

On the whole, when a species died out, it was succeeded by creatures of its own kin. The extinction of the

dinosaurs was different, in that a whole dominant race, inhabiting the world for 200 million years suddenly (in terms of geological time), came to an end, to be succeeded by the warm-blooded mammals and birds.

From the standpoint of the human race the twilight of the dinosaurs lasted a long time, probably some hundreds of thousands of years; but set against the vast background of the earth's history, the end was as sudden

Horned dinosaurs once thundered across the plains over 70 million years ago.

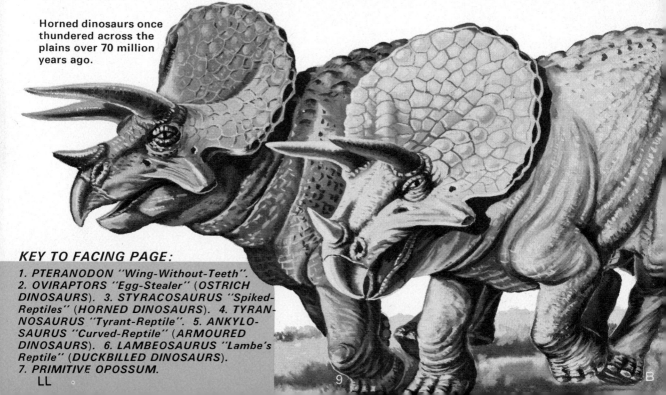

KEY TO FACING PAGE:

1. PTERANODON "Wing-Without-Teeth". 2. OVIRAPTORS "Egg-Stealer" (OSTRICH DINOSAURS). 3. STYRACOSAURUS "Spiked-Reptiles" (HORNED DINOSAURS). 4. TYRAN-NOSAURUS "Tyrant-Reptile". 5. ANKYLO-SAURUS "Curved-Reptile" (ARMOURED DINOSAURS). 6. LAMBEOSAURUS "Lambe's Reptile" (DUCKBILLED DINOSAURS). 7. PRIMITIVE OPOSSUM.

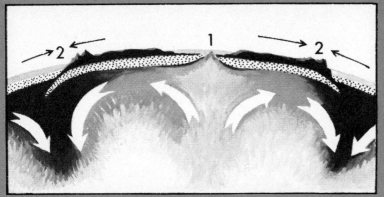

Diagram of the Continental Drift. 1. When "plates" move apart molten rock pushes up to fill the gap. 2. When the plates collide great earth movements fold up mountain ranges.

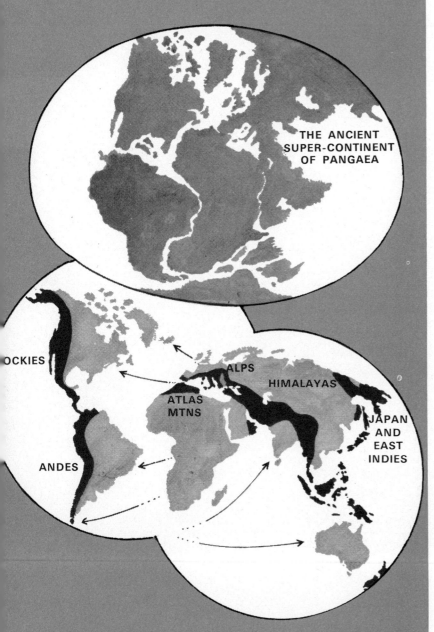

THE ANCIENT SUPER-CONTINENT OF PANGAEA

ROCKIES

ALPS

HIMALAYAS

ATLAS MTNS

JAPAN AND EAST INDIES

ANDES

These maps of the world show some of the great mountain chains which were created through the drifting apart and collisions of Continental masses.

as it was complete.

The closing days of the dinosaurs are dramatically inscribed in certain rock formations in northwest America.

Here the sedimentary layers were found lying evenly on top of one another, showing that they had not been disturbed since they were laid down between a 100 and 70 million years ago.

On the lower levels were found rich boneyards of dinosaurs and other reptile fossils, with here and there a few small fragments of primitive mammals; then came several feet above of barren rock, before a final strata, in which once again were numerous fossil deposits. But here lay a great variety of early mammals and not so much as a dinosaur tooth among them.

It was as though the earth, in burying the great reptiles, had effaced their memory from the ensuing age.

The story unfolded from the rocks points not only to the abruptness of the extinction, but to the mystery of how and why such an end overtook not only the small and great dinosaurs, but the sea-going Plesiosaurs, Mosasaurs and the hordes of gliding Pterosaurs that swarmed in the air.

At the same time, how was it that the doom that overtook so many species of reptile, spared the turtles, snakes, lizards and crocodiles that (as far as the latter were concerned) were closely related to the dinosaurs?

Before going into some of the theories put forward to account for the disappearance of a long-lived, successful race of animals, let us look at the profound changes that took place towards the end of the Cretacious period, when great mountain building was taking place all over the world.

Most scientists today agree that the phenomenon known as Continental Drift is the main cause of the buckling and folding of the earth's surfaces.

We are told that the earth's crust is like an eggshell cracked in several places into pieces or "plates". These "plates", carrying the continents on their backs, float on the heavier rocks of the earth's mantle.

Radioactive elements in the core of our planet are continually melting the underlying rocks, causing them to "boil", much as thick soup does in a saucepan, only at an infinitely slower rate.

These "boilings" are known as *convection currents* and are the powerful forces that move the "plates", so that over millions of years the shape of the world's land masses and seas are altered in their relation to one another.

When continents "collide" or the edge of one "plate" slides under another, great mountain ranges are squeezed up; when continents drift apart oceans and seas are formed.

Towards the end of the Cretacious

period geological changes increased. The North and South Americas separated from Europe and Africa to form the Atlantic Ocean.

At the same time a great chain of mountains rose up along the Pacific side of the Americas to form the Andean and Rocky ranges.

Across the world, India (which had been an island off the coast of East Africa) drifted north and collided with Asia, forcing up the Himalayas; while Africa pressing on Europe, pushed Italy into the mainland thrusting up the Alps. These movements continued on north to Britain, folding the South Downs.

It was in these times of change and upheaval that the dinosaurs played out the last great drama of their existence.

Almost to the end of the Cretacious period the dinosaurs and the reptiles were thriving and powerful. Why then did they vanish from the world they had dominated for a billion years?

The honest answer is—nobody knows!

For the difficulty in solving the problem is to find a cause, or even several inter-related causes, that could have singled out a group of diverse reptiles, yet left untouched some, closely related species, that were living amongst them.

At this point, it might be interesting to look at some of the theories put forward to account for the mass extinction of dinosaurs and see if any can claim to answer the riddle. They are as follows:

(a) The dinosaurs were killed by a cloud of cosmic dust through which the world was passing at that time.

(b) A great epidemic swept them away, or unknown gases from a nearby comet's tail poisoned all the water. Choking by volcanic dust, overwhelming earthquakes or pre-

The Duckbilled dinosaurs were hunted by carnosaurs and needed deep water into which they could escape. But even there they were not safe since the rivers were full of giant crocodiles. Above: a giant phobus crocodile attacks Parasaurolophs.

An Upper Cretacious landscape showing the Pachycephalosaur, a thickheaded dinosaur, and an armoured dinosaur and carnosaur.

Noah floods.

(c) Primitive mammals ate all the dinosaurs' eggs.

(d) Changes in climate interfered with seasonal egg laying, making them infertile.

(e) Changes in food supply killed off the plant-eating dinosaurs, leaving the carnosaurs to starve to death.

(f) The theory of racial old age. This assumes that a race, like an individual, has a limited life-span progressing from infancy, through adolescence to old age and death. According to this theory there is no mystery about the dinosaurian extinction, their end was "built in".

(g) Changes in climate, brought about through the opening up of the Atlantic Ocean and the accompanying uplift of great mountain chains, caused such a drop in the temperature that the dinosaurs froze to death.

The solutions that depend on cosmic clouds, comet or volcanic gas, earthquakes, floods or poisoned water, fail to explain why some species were affected while others escaped.

Epidemics might wipe out a species or two on one continent (as it is thought the vampire bats helped to exterminate the early horses in South America) but it is hardly likely that an epidemic could destroy a world wide race made up of so many differ-

ing species.

The suggestion that early mammals ate up the dinosaurs' eggs faster than they could hatch, runs up against the fact that the mammals were small and few during the great reptiles' heyday, only becoming prominent *after* the dinosaurs had gone.

It should be noticed that crocodiles, turtles and snakes have their eggs eaten today by many kinds of animals, yet they manage to survive.

Interruption in egg laying due to seasonal changes could have had some effect, and French scientists, studying the microstructure of certain fossil eggs, have found signs in the shells indicating a "stop-go" process in the laying of the eggs; a situation that could have arisen if a sudden cold spell had induced torpor in the reptiles.

However, if this were the case, why were other reptiles' eggs not similarly affected?

The change in vegetation, from non-flowering conifers and horsetails to the broad-leaved flowering trees and flowers akin to our times, is a popular reason given for the dying

out of the dinosaurs. The supposition is that the plant-eaters of the Late Cretacious period could not adapt themselves to the change in diet and subsequently died out, depriving the meat-eating dinosaurs of food.

What the adherents of this theory seem to forget is, that the angiosperms —or flowering plants—were evolving throughout the greater part of the Cretacious, so that the herbivorous dinosaurs had plenty of time in which to adjust to the new food plants. The latter-end vigour and diversity of these dinosaurs seems to point rather to their thriving on the vegetation.

In addition many of the meat-eaters lived on lizards and insects and these continued to be abundant up to the present day.

Another popular theory is that of racial old age—or senescence. If races, like individuals have a child-hood to old age life-plan, how is one to account for such hardy old timers as Lampshells, Horseshoe Crabs, Coelacanth fish and the remarkable Tuateras that have lived for hundreds of millions of years in a state of arrested evolution and still show no

signs of change?

Surely it strains credibility to accept that *all* the dinosaurs' life-spans should end aburptly at one point in geological time?

The opening up of the Atlantic and the accompanying mountain orogeny created great changes in the world's climates. Reptiles, being cold-blooded, cannot stand wide variations of hot and cold, so no doubt this contributed to the extermination of dinosaurs in the colder parts of the earth.

But all the theories advanced so far suffer from the same flaw—none of them throws any light on the selective factors that killed off some groups and by-passed other related species.

This is the problem awaiting solution by some future palaeontologists.

It may be in the end, that extinction will be found to be due to a number of subtly interacting causes, some of which are known, and some still to be discovered, that came together at a point in geological time, to destroy the most awesome race ever generated by the fruitful earth—a race which fascinates modern man.

A scene depicting the last days of the dinosaurs.

At Home In The Trees

By Dr. Maurice Burton

The puma, or cougar, often has to find refuge in a tree.

THE puma, or cougar, the so-called mountain lion of America, is a great climber. When hunted by dogs it always shins up a tree as a last resort. Several years ago, when there were numerous reports of a puma roaming the countryside in Surrey, several people claimed to have seen a reddish animal jump down from a tree and supposed it must have been a puma. Investigation made it fairly certain that in all cases the animal concerned was a common red fox.

Inquiries showed that foxes go into trees more than we suspect although their real home is on the ground. It was a surprise to find, therefore, in the course of these inquiries, a fox with its home in a tree 14 feet from the ground. The tree was pollarded, so it had a flat top, but it meant that there were few branches to give a foothold. The fox had to take a running jump at

> When the hunt is on, and the enemy is stealthily stalking its prey, the hunted creature will often take refuge in trees, for there it will find comfort and safety.

the trunk and more or less scrabble its way up. Yet this fox was a vixen and she had her cubs in the refuge at the top of the tree.

There need be little surprise in the tree-climbing habits of the red fox, even though climbing is not a feature of most members of the dog-family, to which foxes belong. There is, in fact, in North America, a tree fox, known as the grey fox. It is only slightly smaller than the red fox, which it resembles closely, except for the readiness with which it will shin up a tree. It usually has its sleeping quarters in a cave but it will quite readily use a hollow trunk for this.

So although neither red nor grey foxes normally make their homes in trees, they show us in a marked way why other animals do so. It is for security. They also suggest how easy it must have been for the first squirrels, monkeys, lemurs, koalas and others that live habitually in

13

trees to have adopted this habit.

For vegetarian animals tree-dwelling gives another advantage. Their food is to hand, the leaves, buds, fruits, bark, even fungi, on which they feed are all around them. Those that choose to vary their diet also have the choice of birds' eggs, or the birds themselves.

If man's very early ancestors lived in trees, as we are often told they did, it is easy now to see the advantages of it.

Some tree-dwelling animals make no nest or home in the accepted sense. They merely go to sleep on a branch or in a fork. Usually such animals have special adaptations for not falling down from the tree in their sleep. Of interest here are the pottos and lorises of Africa and southern Asia respectively. These animals, sometimes called half-monkeys, because they are halfway between lemurs and monkeys, have only a stump for an index finger. This gives them a very wide grip. Their hands are like tongs. So they can cling with a vice-like grip.

Another type of animal, one that lives in trees in South and Central America, is the sloth. It is so much at home in trees that it practically never comes down to ground. On the rare occasions that it does so it can only drag itself along, lying sprawled on the ground, using its claws as grappling hooks.

Its hands and feet look like stumps, the fingers and toes being enclosed in a continuous skin, with the hook-like claws at the end. In the trees the claws are used as hooks to hang upside down from a branch or the sloth may rest with its long arms and legs wrapped round the trunk. It makes no nest, its long shaggy coat being sufficient protection against rain, and it rests 18 hours out of the 24. For the rest of its time it moves about very slowly, eating leaves, flowers and buds.

Most four-legged animals that make their homes in trees sleep in a hollow in the trunk or make a crude

The Tree or Grey fox of North America (above) will often sleep in the hollow trunks of trees. The flying phalanger of Australia sometimes makes his nest in trees.

nest. For many the hole is enough. They do not line it, the soft rotten wood of the decaying interior of the hole forming sufficient mattress. Those living in the colder regions use leaves, especially dead leaves, collected on the ground and carried up into the tree in the mouth. Rotting leaves give out heat and this may be partly the reason they are used.

Some of the lemurs, the relatives of monkeys living in Madagascar, make a nest of twigs and leaves, much in the manner of squirrels. The flying phalangers of Australia, which are the counterpart of flying squirrels elsewhere, sometimes make this kind of nest. It is similar to the familiar tree squirrel's drey, of which the grey squirrel provides many examples.

In winter, when the trees are bare, its dreys are conspicuous. They are massive collections of twigs and leaves perched securely in the forks of branches. No little skill goes into their construction, the twigs being intertwined so that they stand up to the highest winds.

Perhaps the most remarkable aspect of the tree-dwelling four-footed animals is that their nests nowhere compare for workmanship with birds' nests. Yet birds have inferior brains and have only their feet and beaks to use as tools. Even chimpanzees and gorillas with brains and hands very like our own cannot rival birds in their manipulative skill. In any event, they only make sleeping platforms, each animal making a fresh one each night, by bending inwards the twigs and small branches and crudely weaving them.

For sheer impudence we must turn to the longtailed field mice and, more especially, their close relatives, the yellow-necked mice. These normally make their homes in burrows in the ground. Not infrequently, however, one or more will use a small hole in a tree trunk, six feet or more up from the ground, and they have been known to use holes in trees or deserted birds' nests 40 feet or more high in trees. What is more, these mice are inveterate hoarders of berries and nuts, and a yellow-neck, only about the size of two walnuts himself, will carry walnuts high up into a tree to store them.

The lemurs of Madagascar (above) make nests out of twigs and leaves. The long-tailed field mouse (right) loves to hoard nuts and berries in tree-holes which have been deserted by birds such as bullfinches (below).

FEED THE BIRDS

Birds are fascinating creatures, as all bird-watchers know. And one of the most rewarding ways of observing their habits is to attract them to your garden by putting out a feeding table for them.

WOULD you like to attract birds to your garden ? Would you like to see them eating, drinking, and bathing close to you ? Some gardens attract more birds than others. By following a few simple principles you, too, can increase the number and variety of birds that visit your garden.

The first thing to do is to make a bird table. This can be quite a simple affair constructed from a broom handle and a flat piece of wood about two feet square. Just nail the square on to one end of the pole, push the pole into the ground, and there is your bird table.

The table top should be at least four feet from the ground to prevent cats from jumping onto it. It is a good idea to fix inch-high wooden beading around the edges of the table to stop the food from being blown off by the wind. Leave the table top free of beading for a few inches at one corner for cleaning and drainage purposes.

The siting of the table is very important. It should not be too close to trees or bushes for cats will be able to get onto it from above. The distance between the table and bushes or trees should be a minimum of seven feet. Similarly, it should be positioned at least four feet from

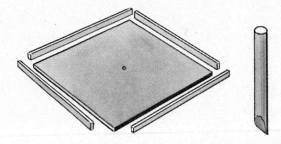

To make your bird table you will need a flat piece of wood, two feet square, and a broom handle. Nail the wood to one end of the pole and then take four strips of beading and nail these round the edges of the wood, leaving a few inches free of beading at one corner so that you have room to clean and drain the table. Then push the pole into the ground.

the house, or indoor activity may frighten away your feathered guests.

Some of the smaller birds, such as the tit family, will prefer a hanging 'table', for these winged acrobats are quite at home upside down or the right way up. Cut a coconut in half and hang it from the branch of a tree. Do not, however, put out coconut during the breeding season as the youngsters cannot digest it. When the coconut is finished the empty shell can still be used as a container for some of the foods described below. If you do not have a coconut, a small tin will do just as well. But be sure that it has no sharp edges.

Always have a bowl of fresh water on the table, or somewhere else where cats cannot get at it. The water in the bowl should be no more than two inches deep. Birds love to bathe and, during the summer months especially, you will get so many bathers at the bowl that the water will soon become extremely murky. It may prove necessary to change the water perhaps two or three times during the day. But try not to disturb the birds when you do this or you may frighten them away for good. During the winter months put luke-warm water in the bowl so that it does not freeze over too quickly. And again, if you can, change the water periodically.

There is a wide variety of foods that you can put out for the birds. You will find that different foods attract different birds. A selection of various foods on your table will bring a wide variety of birds to your garden.

Natural foods like berries and nuts can be collected and put on the table. Hawthorn, elder, berberis, cotoneaster, ivy, and mountain ash are always popular. During the winter months, holly berries and mistletoe berries will be welcome. All types of seed are suitable. Seed can also be stored to provide an ample supply in the winter. Chestnuts, hazel nuts, beech nuts, and so on, can also be stored quite easily.

DO'S AND DONT'S

Congealed fat can be used to bind all manner of kitchen scraps. This 'pudding' can be put on the table, in hanging containers, and wedged in cracks and crevices in trees. Fat, bacon, and suet (*NOT* shredded) are particularly popular. Dog biscuits soaked in milk or water, rice pudding, cooked potato, bread (preferably wholemeal), cake, fruit, in fact almost anything, are all acceptable.
Do NOT put out chocolate, dessicated coconut, shredded suet, or salted nuts as these can cause harm, or even kill. All kitchen scraps should be cleared from the table at the end of each day as they will attract vermin, or go bad.

The amount of food put out should be reduced during the summer months. But do remember—once you start to put out food do it regularly. If you go away for any period ask a friend or a neighbour to do it for you. This is particularly important in the winter when the birds will come to expect it and may depend on you for their continued existence.

You will find your bird table a source of continual interest and enjoyment. And your interest will increase ten-fold if you first equip yourself with a good book on bird recognition so that you can identify your feathered visitors.

A: Berberis

B: Cotoneaster

C: Hazel Nuts

D: Spanish Chestnuts

THE full moon washed the hills and valleys and the forests of northern British Columbia with its golden light.

A soft wind was blowing. It stirred the manes and tails of the band of horses cropping the short blue grass on a hill top.

A little apart from the main band of horses, Royal, a Palomino horse, grazed alone. The moonlight shone on his golden body, and on his silver mane and tail, stirring in the wind. His owner valued him above all his other lovely horses.

Suddenly Royal raised his head, his small inward-curving ears pricked forward. He gave a whistling blast of alarm through his wide, flaring nostrils, and stamped one dainty foot into the thyme-scented turf. His neck was arched and his long tail curved out and down like a silver waterfall.

Four mounted men, dark and menacing in the moonlight, swept down on the horses. In a second the band was thundering downhill. Instinctively Royal took up his responsibilities as the only stallion with the band. At full gallop he waved from flank to flank, nipping at the mares and colts and fillies, bunching them together, forcing them to greater speed.

Once he turned full circle, mane and tail flying, to face his pursuers, blasted his defiance, and turned to fight.

His teeth bared, ears flattened against his head, his neck outstretched, he dashed at the nearest of his pursuers.

The horse thief screamed as Royal came up on his hind legs, flailing downwards with his forefeet, squealing his rage. The man twirled from the saddle and Royal sank his teeth into his pony's neck.

The horse thieves had their lassoes ready, and as Royal released his grip, a wide loop settled over his head. As he reared again, another loop flicked round both forelegs.

They had him. Deft flicks of their roping arms tightened the nooses, as their trained ponies turned to take the strain. Royal fell heavily, his forelegs pulled from beneath him, and he rolled, yet another lasso settling over his threshing hind legs. The horse thieves stretched him out between two ponies, the lasso taut, and on his head they put a war bridle. This was a halter made of the hard rope of a lasso, with a knot on each side of the head. The thing was constructed so that the knots would be pulled tight against the head if Royal resisted.

With two ropes round his neck, and the brutal bridle secured, the men took the lasso from Royal's legs and he struggled to his feet. Screaming with rage he dashed at the nearest mounted man, who had the rope from the bridle snubbed to his saddle horn. But the lasso on his neck tightened immediately, choking

him. Royal stood still, half strangled. The world had turned black. The knots against his head bit into him. They pulled him forward, beating him from behind. If he tried to fight, they choked him. If he refused to move the bridle was tightened.

The thieves led the streaming, mud-caked, sweating horse away through the night. As dawn was breaking, they forced him into a cattle truck. Two hundred miles farther on, they turned him into a corral.

Royal stood in a corner, his head up, his eyes wild. The blood oozed from beneath the war bridle. He would not touch the hay and water put before him.

All that day he stood in the hot sun, and in the cool of the evening the mosquitoes covered him in a grey blanket.

At midnight, Royal hooked himself over the top log of the corral. Half leaping, struggling with all his strength, he slithered over the rough, knotted timber, tearing his hide. He landed in a crumpled heap, but he was free.

He ran off through the night, and the clouds opened. The rain beat down, cold and soothing to his skin, driving the mosquitoes to the ground.

FEAR OF MAN

Day by day, Royal went south, sometimes west. He swam the creeks and rivers which crossed his path. Sometimes he moved along man-made tracks. At other times, he went winding and twisting through the forests on the trails made by moose and deer.

Occasionally he came to small settlements, but although he was attracted by the sight and smell of other horses, he avoided them, for he knew that man was there too, and Royal now lived in fear of man.

Weeks passed, and Royal grew fat and shining with good living. Did he recognise the distant Rockies when they first came into view?

In October, when the forests and hills were brilliant with red and orange, gold and green, Royal whinnied loudly. His whole body shook as he expelled his breath in one great quivering cry of greeting. His pricked ears were pointed at the snow-capped Rockies, as he cantered through the cool.

Royal found his band of horses on the hills. He broke into a racking, springing trot. His head was high and shone with gold and silver in the sunlight.

The band of horses turned to watch his coming. A slim grey filly whinnied softly in welcome, and moved towards him. Royal was "home" once more.

GOLDEN STALLION

THE WONDER OF WOOD

Stop and think for a moment. Think of all the things which you use every day in your life. How many of these things do you think are made of wood? A good many of them, probably, because even in this age of steel, concrete and plastics, wood still has a wide range of important everyday uses.

Go through, in your mind, a typical day in your life to find out how many things you use that are made of wood. When you wake up, for example, perhaps part of the bed you have been sleeping on is made of wood. Walk out of the bedroom into the bathroom, the doors are also made of wood. Downstairs for breakfast. The steps and bannisters, they too, are made of wood. If you continued in that way till the end of the day, you would be amazed at the number of wooden things you do use without realising it. We have grown so accustomed to using wood for so many of our daily needs that it would be very difficult for us to live without it.

Elephants roll logs of teak down to the stream.

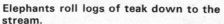

Above: the texture of teak wood. Right: the leaves of the teak are very rough and the flowers hang in loose clusters. Below: Building a ship out of the wood from teak.

TOUGH TEAK

Teak wood is strong, heavy and long-lasting. It comes from a tall tree found in the tropical parts of the world such as Burma, Siam and Ceylon. The trees have to be dried before they are cut down. The tree is deadened by cutting away a large circle of the bark and the outer sapwood. As the heart or centre of the wood dries, which can sometimes take as long as three years, it becomes evenly seasoned and lighter. Then, when it is completely dry, it is cut down. The logs are then cut and they are dragged by specially trained elephants and buffaloes to the nearest stream, and floated down to a nearby town.

Teak is very tough wood. It contains resin or gum which protects it from wood borers and white ants. It is one of the most valued woods for shipbuilding because its surface is very durable and it does not warp.

Above: elmwood. Right: the leaves of the elm. Below: an elmwood jetty.

THE ELEGANT ELM

The wood that comes from one of England's most elegant and best loved trees, the elm, is strong and tough.

It is less likely to split than any other timber and can be cut into larger pieces. It does not rot when damp and keeps in very good condition when permanently wet. For this reason elmwood has a variety of uses.

The wood may be used for making parts of boats, garden furniture, wagons, carts and other constructions that may be exposed to the weather permanently.

Wych elm is perhaps the most useful of all the elms because its wood is very tough and is almost as heavy as oak. It is less troublesome to work than English and Dutch elms which are lighter and tend to warp and twist. Some elmwood is used for decorative designs on furniture.

An elm tree usually grows to a height of 120 feet. Its bark is thick and greyish in colour, and its leaves are oval-shaped and rough textured.

The elm is very vulnerable to disease which comes from a certain form of fungus and when this happens the branches may often fall without warning.

Above: An elm log which will be made into a decorative chair and the wheels of a cart. Below: the branch of a diseased elm comes crashing down to the ground—a near miss for the man who had been enjoying a quiet walk in the park. A word of warning! It is unwise to sit and picnic under an elm tree!

UNBENDABLE BALSA

The word balsa comes from a Spanish word meaning raft because the natives of South America used balsa to make their rafts.

The texture of balsa wood. Planed wood of good quality has a satiny finish.

The balsa tree is one of the fastest-growing of all trees. It is found in the tropical forests of Central America and in parts of South America. The tree grows very rapidly on well-drained moist, rich, soil and reaches 60 to 70 feet in only seven years. The balsa tree has a rather unusual appearance. It has straight trunk and a smooth bark and will only grow well when it is given plenty of sunlight.

The wood of the balsa tree is very light and strong and does not bend easily. After six or seven years the tree is ready for cutting. If it is allowed to grow any more it may become diseased or rotten. When the tree has been cut down and the cells are dead they become filled with air and this makes the wood lighter than cork.

The name 'balsa' comes from a Spanish word which means raft because the word was used by the natives of South America for making their rafts and canoes. Balsa wood was used extensively during World War II in aircraft work, for life-saving rafts, and for buoys. The wings and fuselage of a fighter aircraft, the Mosquito, were made from balsa wood because it is so light and rigid. The wood is also used for making toy model aeroplanes and boats, and for insulating ceilings and walls.

In 1947 Thor Heyerdahl and his five companions made their famous raft for the Kon-Tiki expedition from logs of balsa wood. They used the raft to sail 4,300 miles across the Pacific.

Timber! The time has come to cut down the balsa trees which have grown for six or seven years. If they are allowed to grow any longer they may begin to rot.

Once used for making parts of a fighter aircraft, balsa wood is now used for making toy model aeroplanes and boats.

SOLID OAK

The wood from oak trees has been used by men for hundreds of years in the building of ships, houses, ladders, and wheel spokes. The Romans used it to build their ships with, because the wood is exceedingly strong and heavy.

Sailing ships of all kinds, from small fishing boats, to men-of-war, were built of oak heartwood shaped by hand before power saws and sawmills developed. The heartwood of oak has a warm, rich, dark brown colour and is extremely durable.

Oak makes excellent fencing timber and has also been used for the making of all kinds of furniture for years.

Oak branchwood is a very good source of fuel. It can also be made into good quality charcoal. Even the bark has its uses. The bark contains tannin and was for centuries used in the leather and tanning industry.

Oak has so many uses, that it is perhaps the most important of all the trees.

Oak trees have always been a familiar sight in the country.

Above: the beautiful texture of oakwood. Right: the wavy-edged leaves and acorns of the oak tree.

Above left: a beautiful piece of furniture carved out of oakwood. Above right: Stout, straight logs are used at the sawmill. Below: The wonderful sailing ships of days gone by were made of heartwood oak.

Nature Quiz

Now you have read the nature section of this book, see how many of the questions you can answer in the quiz below. The answers are at the back of the book.

1 Some very strange creatures of the animal kingdom are found in the East. One of these has a remarkable tail that reaches an amazing length by growing at the rate of three feet a year. What is this creature called?

2 Kissing gourami fish have some very unusual habits. They feed by means of a pair of protruding lips, and are equipped with special breathing apparatus which helps them to breathe under water containing no oxygen. Where are these fish found?

3 Why does the sac fish blow up its stomach into a huge balloon-like bag?

4 The Malayan tapir has a large snout which makes its head look like that of an elephant's. How does this creature escape from its enemies?

5 One peculiar creature gets its name from the shape of its nose and its fondness for a certain food. What is it called?

6 These elegant creatures dine on nuts and fruit and can cover a distance of 60 to 80 feet in one long leap. What are they called?

7 Why is the proboscis monkey so called?

8 This bird was supreme among the supernatural beings worshipped by the Red Indians of North America. It had eyes that flashed lightning and beating wings which rolled thunder. What was this terrifying bird called?

9 The very earliest gods of ancient Egypt were all represented as birds or animals. Gradually these took on the form of gods. Why was the hawk held so sacred by the ancient Egyptians?

10 Perhaps the most famous of all mythical creatures, this bird cremated itself every 500 years and arose rejuvenated out of its own ashes. Its name has passed into our language as a symbol of rebirth. What is this bird called?

11 In the Rime of the Ancient Mariner a bird brings a curse on the ship. Which bird was it?

12 Why is the chough protected in Cornwall?

13 It is an unquestionable fact that the last dinosaur perished many millions of years ago. Do you know exactly how many million years ago?

14 For how many years did dinosaurs inhabit the world?

15 Dinosaurs became extinct at the close of which Period?

16 How did their extinction differ from that of other species?

17 Trees are very good hiding places for hunted animals. When the enemy is prowling about in search of its prey many animals will scamper up trees to take refuge among the leaves. The Tree or Grey fox will often sleep in the hollow trunks of trees. Where does the Tree fox live?

18 The long-tailed field mouse has another use for trees. What habit is this creature renowned for?

19 Teak wood comes from tall trees which are found in what parts of the world?

20 Teak is a very tough wood. What is the name of the substance that protects teak from wood pests?

21 Why is it particularly valued for ship-building?

22 When the centre of a teak tree has dried it becomes lighter, and when it is completely dry it is cut down. The logs have then to be taken to the nearest river and floated down stream to a town. What animals are used for dragging the teak logs to streams?

23 The elm is one of England's finest and most elegant trees. To what height does it usually grow?

24 One kind of elm wood is less troublesome to work than Dutch and English elm, because it is very tough and does not warp. Which type of elm is this?

25 Where do balsa trees grow?

26 How long does it take for them to grow to a height of 60 to 70 feet?

27 What does the word "balsa" mean, and why is it so-called?

28 In 1947 Thor Heyderdahl and his five companions made their famous Kon-Tiki expedition across the Pacific Ocean. What has balsa wood to do with this expedition?

29 The advantage of balsa wood is that it is both light and rigid. This is why it was used in making aircraft. What makes this wood so light?

30 The oak is one of man's most useful trees. Even its branches and bark have their uses. There are two very important things which we obtain from branchwood. What are they?

OUR WONDERFUL WORLD OF SCIENCE

LOOK, NO HANDS!

THE STORY OF AUTOMATIC GUIDANCE IN THE AIR

THE words "automatic pilot", "blind landing" and "guided missile" all have a modern ring about them, but like a great number of scientific inventions all these ideas and devices have their roots much further back in history than one imagines. Already in 1912, just nine years after the Wright Brothers' first flights, a far-sighted American engineer, Elmer Sperry, was working on ways to take some of the burden of a long, difficult flight off the pilot's shoulders. He produced the world's first autopilot, and today the company he founded is still one of the foremost in the business.

The illustrations on this page show some of the milestones in the history of automatic flight:—

A. A guided missile of 1915! One of the Sperry autopilot-controlled aircraft built for the U.S. Navy as "aerial torpedoes".

B. The Boeing 247 which made the first automatic landing of all—in England, in 1944.

C. The North American F-86D "Sabre Dog", first all-weather fighter equipped to detect, lock-on to and destroy enemy aircraft while its pilot sat and watched, monitoring the attack only.

D. The BEA Hawker Siddeley Trident 1 which made the first ever automatic touchdown on a commercial airline service, at London Heathrow Airport on June 10, 1965.

E. A "Smart Bomb" being released from an American fighter bomber. This weapon steers itself onto any pinpoint target indicated to it.

F. From blast-off to splashdown the Apollo moonflights made much use of computer-controlled automatic manoeuvring.

G. Teledyne-Ryan AQM-91A air-launched drones (pilotless aircraft) used by the U.S. Air Force for reconnaissance over enemy territory.

FIRST AIRCRAFT WITH
SPERRY AUTOPILOT, 1912

DOOLITTLE

QUEEN BEE

BOEING 247

TRANSATLANTIC DC-4

DIAL 'S' FOR SPIN

WHEN in 1912 Elmer A. Sperry of the Sperry Gyroscope Company put together a collection of gyros, springs, counterweights and linked them to a biplane's controls he produced the first rudimentary auto-pilot—a device able to keep the aircraft on a straight and level course, in smooth weather or turbulence. Its 1970s off-spring can bring a giant airliner smooth-ly down to the ground for a feather-light touchdown, and steer it along the runway with the pilots only monitoring their controls and equipment.

In the early years of flying the pilot's main enemy was the weather. The pioneers, by skill and cunning, could find their way through snow, ice and fog, but to open up the large-scale future for air transport it was necessary to take the adventure out of it and replace it with all-weather reliability. The equipment inside the cockpit and on the ground had to be improved so that the pilot could fly accurately in any conditions.

The first dramatic demonstration of "blind flying" was given by the famous Jimmy Doolittle on September 24, 1929. Completely enclosed under a hood in the rear cockpit of a special radio-equipped Consolidated NY-2 bi-plane he took off from Mitchell Field, Long Island, flew a 15 mile course and returned to land relying entirely on the instruments in the cockpit.

As science progressed the ILS or Instrument Landing System was born, and is still used today. Radio beams transmitted from near the runway on the ground activated an instrument displayed in the cockpit, a dial bearing two white bars, one vertical, one hori-zontal. The pilot manipulated his controls and engine throttles to keep the two bars centred to make a perfect cross on the centre of the dial and thus knew that he was heading straight for the runway and descending at the correct angle to meet it.

While these advances in safety and reliability went on, a new breed of

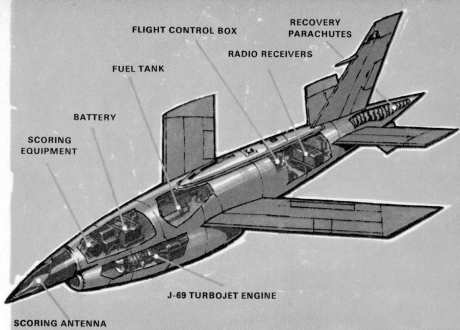

FLIGHT CONTROL BOX

RECOVERY PARACHUTES

RADIO RECEIVERS

FUEL TANK

BATTERY

SCORING EQUIPMENT

J-69 TURBOJET ENGINE

SCORING ANTENNA

FIREBEE

SABRE DOG

RPV PILOTS

aircraft was produced to meet military needs. To give Army and Navy gunners realistic flying targets, "drone" or pilotless planes were designed, radio-controlled from the ground.

In the 1930's many types were produced, notably in Britain the Queen Bee (a pilotless De Havilland Tiger Moth) and the Airspeed Queen Wasp. Gunnery was not good enough to make this an expensive business—one story tells of a demonstration before some very high-ranking visitors during which half an hour's concentrated blazing away by all guns left the drone target untouched. To avoid embarrassment the officer controlling the plane was quietly told to dial the appropriate code signals to put it into a spin and crash it!

The development of autopilots and the ILS equipment proceeded separately, and the idea of coupling them together so that the aircraft could fly *itself* down to land was first tried out in October 1944 at the telecommunications flying unit based at Defford in Worcestershire. The aircraft was a Boeing 247, and from the flights it made all modern automatic landings have developed.

In 1947 another dramatic event occurred. A Douglas C-54 Skymaster of the U.S. Army Air Force's all-weather flying centre flew 2,400 miles from Newfoundland to England under full automatic control. It carried a crew of nine but they did not touch the controls once during the $10\frac{1}{4}$ hour flight.

In the 1950's an all-weather fighter emerged which could find and destroy enemy intruders without its pilot ever seeing them. This was the North American F-86D, nicknamed "Sabre Dog", which with the development of radar and computers compact enough to fit into a single-seat fighter was the first of a string of deadly hunters. Once the radar was locked onto its target the 'plane positioned itself for an attack, fired its rocket weapons and then warned the pilot when to break away!

As fighters and their weapons advan-

ced so did the need for realistic targets for training. Most famous of these jet-age targets, which accurately represent the speed and flight characteristics of an "enemy", are the Ryan Firebee family and the Jindiviks used over the test ranges at Woomera in Australia. The automatic control systems of these pilotless 'planes are very advanced.

There are now whole families of RPV's—Remotely Piloted Vehicles—which, air-launched from mother planes, are sent high or low over enemy territory controlled by a pilot who is hundreds of miles away in safety, and whose "eyes" are TV cameras carried on the aircraft. At present these drones are used to bring back photographs of enemy territory or transmit back TV pictures directly, but the final step is just around the corner—the RPV's are being developed for use as fighters, bombers and ECM (electronic countermeasures) aircraft designed to confuse and jam an enemy's radar defences, all with pilots who are far away!

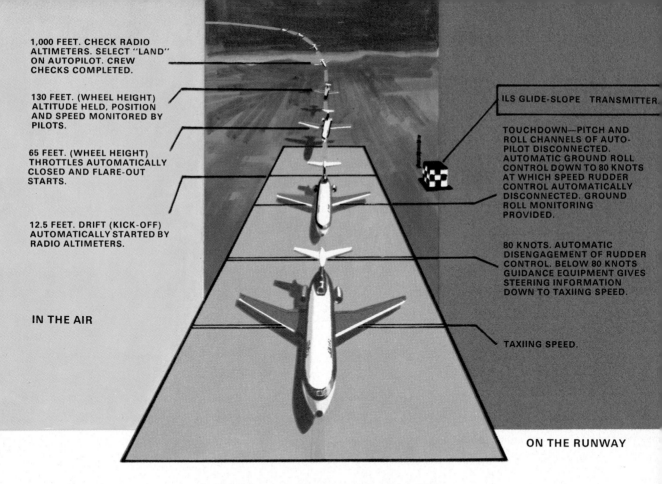

1,000 FEET. CHECK RADIO ALTIMETERS. SELECT "LAND" ON AUTOPILOT. CREW CHECKS COMPLETED.

130 FEET. (WHEEL HEIGHT) ALTITUDE HELD, POSITION AND SPEED MONITORED BY PILOTS.

65 FEET. (WHEEL HEIGHT) THROTTLES AUTOMATICALLY CLOSED AND FLARE-OUT STARTS.

12.5 FEET. DRIFT (KICK-OFF) AUTOMATICALLY STARTED BY RADIO ALTIMETERS.

IN THE AIR

ILS GLIDE-SLOPE TRANSMITTER.

TOUCHDOWN—PITCH AND ROLL CHANNELS OF AUTO-PILOT DISCONNECTED. AUTOMATIC GROUND ROLL CONTROL DOWN TO 80 KNOTS AT WHICH SPEED RUDDER CONTROL AUTOMATICALLY DISCONNECTED. GROUND ROLL MONITORING PROVIDED.

80 KNOTS. AUTOMATIC DISENGAGEMENT OF RUDDER CONTROL. BELOW 80 KNOTS GUIDANCE EQUIPMENT GIVES STEERING INFORMATION DOWN TO TAXIING SPEED.

TAXIING SPEED.

ON THE RUNWAY

AUTOLAND

THE eventual aim of all the years of work on civil airliner automatic landing systems is very simple to describe—it is to allow an aircraft full of passengers to descend to the runway, land and taxi to a halt in its designated parking area without the pilots being able to see out of the cockpit at any time. When this is achieved it will be possible to carry out scheduled airline services with no diversions or delays caused by bad weather. (The airport safety system must, of course, have the same capability, to deal with accidents which occur in bad visibility on the ground.)

Civil flying is controlled by the most rigid and detailed safety regulations in the world and the International Civil Aviation Organisation (ICAO) has laid down a series of very clear requirements for Autoland performance. These range from Category 1—'Operation down to a pilot's decision-to-land height of 200 ft. (60m) with a visibility of more than 2,600 ft. (800m)', to the final category 3c—'Operation down to and along the runway without external visibility'—the definition we started with.

The scientists and engineers setting out to develop automatic landing systems gave themselves a very tough reliability target to reach—known as the "10^7 principle", meaning that in any flights relying on fully automatic landing systems no serious failure should occur more than once in every 10^7 (10 million) flights. This means that each piece of electronic equipment must be utterly reliable and in fact most systems are triplicated—which means there are three separate sets of identical equipment all operating at the same time.

THREE CHANNELS

The Hawker Siddeley Trident 3B fleet of BEA uses such a system—the Smiths Autoland—and is cleared to operate down to ICAO category 3a—'operation down to and along the runway with a minimum external visibility during the final landing phase of 700 ft. (200m)'—such a landing is shown in the diagram above. The triplicated system has three autopilot channels driving three sets of powered controls through three independent hydraulic systems, each driven by one of the three engines. The aircraft's engine throttles are automatically controlled, as is steering guidance along the runway after touchdown. By 1974 the system is expected to be fitted in all 64 of BEA's Tridents.

Military blind autolandings, with simple one-channel systems, became routine for R.A.F. V-Bombers as long ago as 1956, and in January 1970 the R.A.F.'s fleet of 10 Short Belfast long-range freighters became the first military transports in the world to be cleared for "hands-off" automatic landings under everyday operational conditions.

BELFAST

FIRE IT AND FORGET IT!

SPERRY AERIAL TORPEDO

LARYNX

LONG before the radio-controlled targets of the 1930's, experiments were being made with so-called "aerial targets" whose official name concealed the fact that they were the first crude attempts to produce a guided missile to bombard enemy trenches and other targets.

The Sperry-Delco biplane, demonstrated to the U.S. Navy in 1915-16, was powered by a 40 H.P. Ford engine, and controlled in the air by a gyroscope and a height-sensing aneroid barometer. The launching crew had to estimate the target's distance and the effect of any crosswind, then set the engine to cut out over the target. The missile ran along a rail track, took off and headed for the target. When the engine cut out the wing attachment bolts were automatically pulled out and the fuselage with its 300 lb. bomb fell onto the target— they hoped !

The U.S. Army equivalent was the "Kettering Bug", and in Britain Professor A. M. Low worked on little radio-controlled missile biplanes during 1914-17.

INFAMOUS BOMBS

In the 1920's a tiny monoplane missile named "Larynx" was successfully tested over the sea off the south-west coast of Britain—its strange name derived from its long range and lynx engine—but the incredibly potent modern missile had its origin with the infamous pulse jet-engined flying bomb known as the V-1 (Vergeltungswaffe-1 or Revenge Weapon) designed by the German Fieseler Company. Launched from a long ramp it had a crude guidance system which worked (like its remote 1915 ancestors) by engine cut-off over the target. The cut-off was initiated by a mileage counter or by a radio ranging transmitter operating through a 400 ft. aerial trailed by the bomb in flight.

Next came the equally notorious V-2,

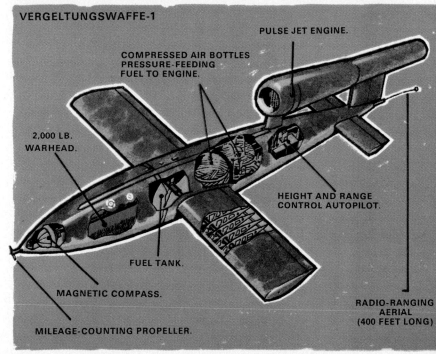

VERGELTUNGSWAFFE-1

PULSE JET ENGINE.

COMPRESSED AIR BOTTLES PRESSURE-FEEDING FUEL TO ENGINE.

2,000 LB. WARHEAD.

HEIGHT AND RANGE CONTROL AUTOPILOT.

FUEL TANK.

MAGNETIC COMPASS.

RADIO-RANGING AERIAL (400 FEET LONG)

MILEAGE-COUNTING PROPELLER.

V-2 (TEST)

DORNIER 217 RELEASES FRITZ-X

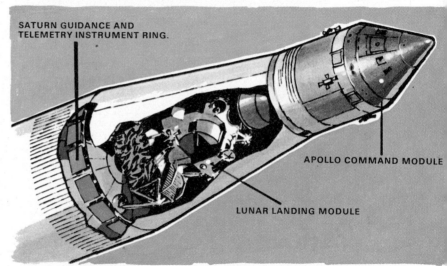

SATURN GUIDANCE AND TELEMETRY INSTRUMENT RING.

APOLLO COMMAND MODULE

LUNAR LANDING MODULE

SATURN ROCKET GUIDANCE

a 46 ft. rocket first test-fired successfully on October 3, 1942. This was the first weapon to reach out to the fringes of space, accelerating to 3,500 m.p.h. and soaring 60 miles up at the top of its trajectory. The guidance system used a three-axis gyroscope autopilot which steered the missile through graphite vanes set in the rocket exhaust and aerodynamic control surfaces on its four stabilising fins.

The German missile-men developed many other rocket missiles none of which, luckily, reached service. One which did in small numbers was the guided bomb, steered onto its target by the bomb-aimer in the launching 'plane. One of these weapons, the 11 ft. long PC-1400X, code-named Fritz-X, demonstrated its terrifying accuracy on the afternoon of September 9th, 1943 when a crack group of Dornier 217K-2 bombers tracked down the Italian fleet

sailing to surrender to the Allies. A Fritz-X released at 18,000 ft. was steered smack into the foredeck of the 42,500 tons battleship *Roma*. It sank in 20 minutes.

After the war the German scientists, their hardware and their research studies were spirited away to form the basis of Russian and American rocketry —from which came the moon landings, the batteries of bombing missiles waiting in their protected sites across two continents, and the incredible undersea weapons like the American Polaris and Poseidon.

ON COURSE

All these rockets, including the towering Saturn moon-launcher with its 7½ million pounds of thrust, have very precise guidance systems to direct

them on course, the basis of which is an inertial device which measures precisely accelerations in any direction. This unit is told where it is starting from and where it is to go, and uses these two pieces of information together with its sensing of all movements after take-off to guide the vehicle to its destination.

The design of guidance systems is nowhere more difficult than in air-to-air missiles which are restricted in size and weight. The most common target for these missiles is the heat from the enemy's jet engine exhaust detected and locked-onto by infra-red radiation sensors. The British Firestreak and Red Top, and the American Sidewinder use this technique. The missile is fired when the pilot's display indicates that its sensors are "seeing" the target, its rocket engine accelerates it rapidly and the sensing head electronics pass commands to the steering fins until proxi-

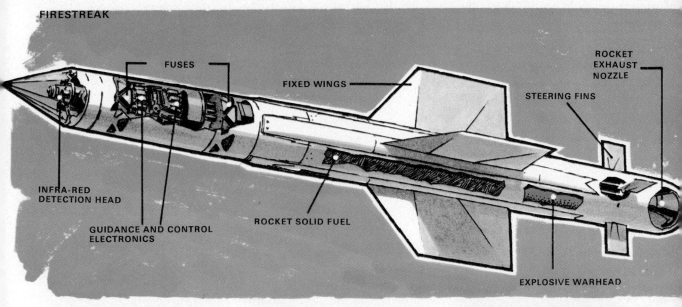

FIRESTREAK

FUSES

FIXED WINGS

ROCKET EXHAUST NOZZLE

STEERING FINS

INFRA-RED DETECTION HEAD

GUIDANCE AND CONTROL ELECTRONICS

ROCKET SOLID FUEL

EXPLOSIVE WARHEAD

LASER-GUIDED WEAPON

BOEING SRAM

SPACE SHUTTLE

mity fuses sense the target and trigger the warhead's explosion.

Another guidance method for ground, sea or air-launched missiles is radar command, one radar tracking the target, another tracking the missile after launch. A computer compares the two lines of flight and ensures that they will collide.

ON TARGET

The latest automatic guidance techniques use television and laser beams. Missiles such as Martel and Condor carry nose-mounted TV cameras, which transmit a picture back to the operator. Once the TV picture shows the target the missile is locked on and steers itself to impact. In a similar manner the head of a laser-guided weapon is equipped to sense the reflections of a laser beam aimed at the target and steer itself

precisely to the spot indicated to it. This system has produced the so-called "smart bomb" which will destroy targets like bridges and pipelines which defy anything but a direct hit. Once locked onto the target these weapons allow the pilot to "fire and forget"—to break away from a sky full of shells and ground-to-air defensive missiles over the target.

The ultimate in such weapons is the "stand-off" bomb—a missile which can be launched hundreds of miles from its target. The newest and deadliest of these is the Boeing SRAM (Short Range Attack Missile) which, only 14 ft. long and 18 inches in diameter, carries a nuclear warhead and a guidance system that steers it accurately for nearly 100 miles in any one of a series of trajectories, high altitude or ground-hugging. Its rocket engine accelerates it to three

times the speed of sound and it is virtually undetectable until it strikes.

An exciting development which combines the space rocket with the aircraft and involves much automatic guidance is the space shuttle, designed in America to boost cargo into space and then return after re-entry to land like a giant glider and be ready two weeks later to go into orbit again. Much of its flight will be controlled by computers and autopilots—with, as always, human pilots watching over them all the time.

MAN ON THE MOVE

One of the penalties man has to suffer in his quest for quicker travel. A giant jet roars over houses near Heathrow Airport.

WHEN any of us feel like visiting some friends or relatives today, even though they might live a hundred miles or more away, we know we can reach them quickly and safely. Transport is no problem, and to reach our destination we would probably have the choice of travelling by rail or road, or both if we wished.

We would certainly not need to make elaborate plans for the journey. A bus ride to the nearest station, perhaps; a few strides to the ticket office, and a walk on to the platform to board the train would be all the effort required.

Moving from place to place today is relatively simple and taken for granted, but of course, it has not always been so. Barely 150 years ago—about six generations—most people lived in isolated communities, seldom venturing beyond the outskirts of their villages. They often lived and died in the houses in which they were born, and only in the most exceptional cases did a few wealthy members of the aristocracy travel farther than just across the English Channel.

Methods of transport in the early 19th century were slow, cumbersome and uncomfortable. Nobody made a long journey unless it was absolutely necessary, and journeys which today are measured in hours, took days or even weeks to complete. It is only in the last 80 to 100 years that man has become really mobile.

First he needed to find ways of transporting materials rather than himself. It was more important to bring in the harvest from the fields, and carry the few simply produced goods, than to visit distant places. Just as we have to learn to walk before we can run, so the early pioneers of transport made slow and inefficient vehicles at first. And just as running comes fairly easily once you have learned to walk, so it was with the transport men and their machines. Once they had discovered a new, basic method of transport, development and improvement came rapidly and suddenly.

★   ★   ★

A tremendous impetus was given to transport with the coming of the Industrial Revolution in Britain which transformed life in this country during the 18th and 19th centuries. The new, mass-produced goods that began to pour out daily from the ever increasing number of factories had to be carried not only to other parts of the country, but also to Europe and elsewhere. The existing methods of transport were neither fast enough nor efficient enough to meet the needs of the machine age. Necessity was, therefore, very much the mother of invention in the field of transport.

Man has made more progress in science and technology in the century or so since the Industrial Revolution than at any other time in his history, and the improvement in transport is a typical example of the advances he has made. Who, even twenty years ago, would have believed that men would be able to travel into outer space, and even land on the Moon? It was the sort of thing people read about in science-fiction novels, but now it is fact.

Let us take a look at one of the earliest forms of transport—the boat. The luxury liner of today is a far cry from the first "ship", which was simply a crude raft of logs. Like other early forms of transport, rafts were not very efficient. It took Man more than a thousand years to increase his speed on the sea, first with the invention of the oar, followed by the sail and then the rudder.

For hundreds of years sailing ships ruled the waves. They reached

Today, British Leyland "minis" are produced by the million, and cars
are no longer the coveted possessions of the very wealthy few, as they
were before mass-production reduced manufacturing costs.

their peak of development with the fast three-masted merchant ships called "clippers" which were built in the middle of the 19th century. With the invention of the steam engine, and its adaption to ships, it seemed almost overnight that sail gave way to steam, bringing big changes for travellers who wanted to go abroad.

In the year 1800, a family seeing their son off to India would not expect to hear news of his safe arrival until a year had elapsed. After the introduction of steamships, followed by the cutting of the Suez Canal in 1896, the voyage to India took only six weeks!

★　★　★

The first steam-powered vessels were made of wood and their engines drove paddle-wheels. Soon the propeller replaced the paddle-wheel, and ships' hulls were built of steel. Coal was replaced by oil as a fuel, marine turbine engines were invented, and diesel engines too, were used to power quite large ships.

Water transport passed a significant milestone in 1959 when the first man-carrying hovercraft, the 3½

ton SR-NI was successfully tested. Hovercraft, or Air Cushion Vehicles as they are sometimes called, were the invention of British engineer Sir Christopher Cockerell. They can carry passengers and cargo over both land and water, skimming along a few feet above the surface.

Hovercraft do not need either harbours or airfields, and can go almost anywhere so long as the surfaces are not too uneven. Because they are not handicapped by the "drag" effect of water on their hulls like a conventional ship, hovercraft can travel at high speeds. The large Mountbatten class hovercraft, SR-N4, which was launched in 1968, could carry 63½ tons at speeds approaching 80 m.p.h.

The movement of men and materials on land was transformed with the coming of the railways. The Cornishman, Richard Trevithick designed the first steam engine in 1801, and built a locomotive to run on an iron tramway connecting an ironworks at Pennydarren with the Glamorganshire Canal —a distance of ten miles—in 1804.

It was 25 years later, however, before the first really successful railway locomotive appeared. This was George Stephenson's "Rocket", which travelled

at a speed of 29.1 m.p.h. in 1829. By the following year the Railway Age had really begun. Railway systems began to spread all over Britain, and the great era of steam which was to last for more than a hundred years, gave people the opportunity to travel all over the country.

★　★　★

But the era of steam was to end suddenly yet almost imperceptibly. The great steam engines disappeared from the tracks as diesel engines began rapidly to replace them in 1955. Since the introduction of diesel and electric trains, speeds by rail have increased. In Japan the Bullet Train whizzes across 320 miles of land in just over three hours, at an average speed of over 100 miles an hour.

And what about those early pioneers of flight? In 1890 a French inventor, Clement Ader made history by leaving the ground for a few seconds in his steam-driven machine. Only twelve years later, Orville and Wilbur Wright had developed a practical biplane glider that could be balanced and controlled in every direction.

34

The first "Mountbatten" class passenger ferry hovercraft (SR.N4) was launched on the sea for the first time in 1968.

The inventor, Sir Christopher Cockerell.

In the following year, 1903, on December 17th they made the world's first true powered, sustained, and controlled flights in a 12-horse power engined biplane which had two propellers. By 1905 they had made the world's first practical aeroplane which could be banked, circled, and flown easily for half-an-hour at a time.

The two World Wars had the effect of accelerating progress and development in aviation. In 1930, the first jet engine was patented by the British engineer Frank Whittle, and the world's first jet aircraft, Germany's Heinkel He-178, flew in 1939.

After the Second World War much attention was given to the jet-propelled plane, and the maximum speeds of such aircraft increased rapidly until, in 1947, the sound barrier was broken by an American jet plane Bell X5-1. And yet only a few years before, aeronautical experts had said that no plane would ever fly faster than sound!

The first jet plane to go into commercial service was the British de Havilland Comet which began flying in 1952. Only seventeen years later, the world saw the first flights of such monsters of the air as the Boeing 747. When this,

the first Jumbo jet, thundered across the sky at a speed of 509 miles an hour in 1969, a new and exciting age of jet travel began. In the same year the Anglo-French supersonic jet Concorde and the Russian equivalent, the Tu 144 made their historic flights, heralding a new era of supersonic travel.

Nowhere is the speed of scientific advance more evident than in Man's dramatic move away from his native Earth and into Space. Only eight years after Yuri Gagarin made history as the first man to be sent into orbit round the Earth in his Russian craft Vostok 1, the American spacecraft Apollo 11 landed on the Moon on July 20th 1969.

★ ★ ★

Whatever happened to man's own physical means of transport, his legs? Hundreds of years ago nomadic tribes travelled on foot with all their worldly possessions carried on their backs. Using pack animals eased the burden a little, but it was not until the invention of the wheel, and afterwards, the improvements to roads, that goods could be transported more efficiently.

Once two-wheeled and four-wheeled

wagons had been developed, stage coaches designed for long-distance travel were introduced. But all these forms of transport still relied on animals for power to drive them.

It was not until 1886 that Karl Benz built the first motor-powered car. It had three wheels and was driven by a petrol engine of ¾ horsepower. This enabled the car to reach the then fantastic speed of 9½ miles an hour. But only thirteen years later, in 1899, Camille Jenatzy's electric car *La Jamais Contente* became the first car to travel at over 60 miles an hour. In October, 1970 the American land speed record breaker, Gary Gabelich reached 100 times that speed when he drove his rocket-propelled *Blue Flame* at the incredible speed of 627.07 miles an hour!

Nowadays cars are being produced daily to meet the needs of the motorist. When Henry Ford, the American car manufacturer, set up his own business in 1903, he became the first person to produce cars cheaply by mass-production. Today, British Leyland minis are produced by the million, and cars are no longer the coveted possession of the very wealthy few.

★   ★   ★

What about transport in the future? What will men be moving in or on in the years to come? On the roads, we may be driving cars with a special guidance system along electronic roads. In the year 2001 we may be able to Dial-a-Route, get into our cars, and be driven to our destination.

Diesel and electric trains may soon vanish to make way for trains that float above the rails, and are pushed along by a powerful invisible force called magnetic levitation. Cockerell's air cushion principle, which has already proved so successful with the Hovercraft, has also been tested on fixed tracks. These Hovertrains which will carry goods and passengers will attain speeds of up to 300 miles an hour.

Scientists are at the moment experimenting with surface effect ships which are a cross between hovercrafts and hydrofoils and will be capable of 100 miles an hour.

In the field of space exploration, the rockets which are now being used to send men into outer space are only the forerunners of more efficient means of propulsion in space. Vehicles driven by atomic power will probably be the next step, and the possibilities of "photon" rockets which will be able to travel at very nearly the speed of light (more than 186,000 miles per second!) are already being investigated.

Whatever form our methods of transport will take in the future, you may be sure that we will all be on the move much faster than we are now. So fasten you safety belts, and sit tight!

Transport of the future. Above: the French Aerotrain which runs on a mono-rail. Below: the Mini-Rover, a rubber-tyred, tracked transporter which will carry 12 passengers.

Human blood cells are like ships carrying vital cargoes of food and oxygen to all parts of the body, sailing through 50,000 miles of veins and arteries.

THE RIVER OF LIFE

THE captains of modern super-tankers might be surprised if they knew more about the strange relationships which exist between their ships and the blood flowing through their own bodies.

If a single blood cell were as large as a super-tanker

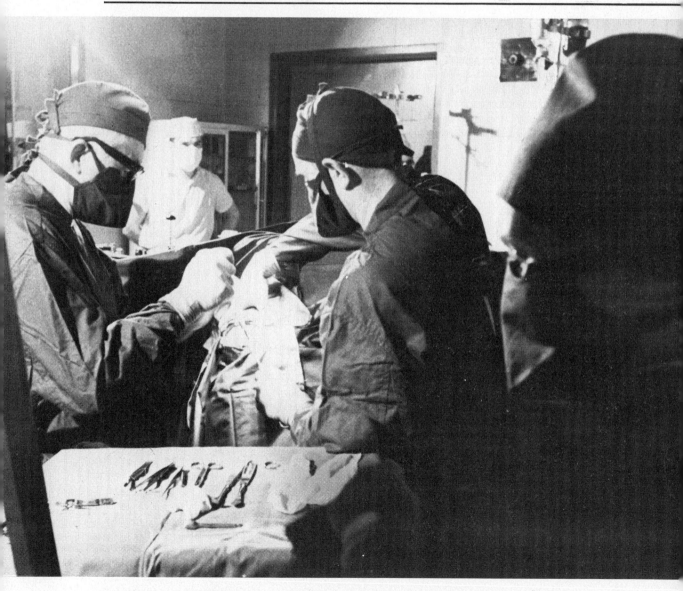

While the heart is methodically pumping blood around a patient's body during an operation, its rhythm is carefully monitored to ensure the patient's safety.

and the body was as big as the world, the journey a blood cell would make to travel just once around the body would be about the same distance as a super-tanker's voyage around the world.

It can take up to two years to design and build a super-tanker, and not many of them are built each year. Yet in the human body more than 9,000,000 blood cells are built *each second* inside bone marrow, and in the spleen, the tonsils, and other glands. Just about as many cells die or are 'scrapped' by the body in the same length of time.

There are probably as many blood cells in the body as there are stars in all the galaxies astronomers observe through their largest telescopes. In a single small drop of blood there are at least 5,000,000 cells. Most of these are called *erythocytes,* or red cells. Blood is red because the erythocytes are red, and the colour is caused by the compound or iron called *haemaglobin.*

In recent years scientists have carefully analysed the chemical nature of haemoglobin, and made large-scale models of haemaglobin molecules.

Shaped like tiny saucers with thick edges and thin centres, the red cells are pumped by the heart through the lungs, where the haemaglobin in the cells combines with oxygen to form a new compound called *oxyhaemaglobin.*

The precious oxygen cargo is then carried to the cells of the body through the arteries. The body cells unload the oxygen and replace it with a new cargo of carbon dioxide, which is then taken back to the lungs through the veins where it is breathed out.

The colour of blood is caused by the compound of iron called haemaglobin. Scientists have made large-scale models of haemaglobin molecules, like that shown here.

The heart is an amazing machine, and somehow puts our space ships and electronic computers to shame. Every single day it pumps more than 1,000 gallons of blood through the body, and it can keep on doing this for a lifetime.

The complicated system of veins and arteries is necessary because of the many jobs the blood has to do. The blood cells must visit different parts of the body to pick up cargoes, and then move on to unload them.

LOADING AND UNLOADING

Blood passes through the walls of the stomach and intestines, loading cargoes of sugar and complicated chemicals called *amino acids,* which are used by the cells when they are unloaded.

It is curious that we go to such lengths to prepare and eat relatively complicated foods which the cells of the body simply could not use. The stomach must first of all *digest* these foods, which really means breaking them down into a few chemicals. We could survive just as easily by swallowing tablets of these few chemicals every day instead of eating. We should be perfectly healthy, but life would then become very dull indeed.

People have been given blood transfusions ever since the 17th century, but the doctors never seemed to know whether the patients would die or not. It was not until 1900 that the blood types of A, B, and O were discovered by the Austrian doctor Karl Landsteiner. Today we know of another type, the AB. Still other types are being discovered but their nature is still not fully understood.

People with type O blood are called 'universal donors' and their blood can be given to anybody. People with type AB blood are known as 'universal recipients' and can take blood from anybody. People with blood types A and B can only give blood to people with the same type.

Besides the red cells there are the white cells or *leucocytes* which are outnumbered by red cells by about 700 to 1. The red cells are the body's cargo ships, but the white cells are the warships which are used to fight disease.

White cells are tiny colourless blobs of a clear jelly-like material called *cytoplasm,* about twice as large as red cells.

ANTI-BODIES

A white cell is actually a single-celled living thing in its own right. Like the tiny single-celled *amoeba* found in pond water, a white cell can surround tiny particles and absorb them into its body. When an infection starts up in some part of the body extra numbers of white cells are rushed to the scene, and the cells busily start surrounding and destroying disease germs.

The 'sea' in which blood cells float is a pale yellow liquid called *plasma,* which is about 90 percent water. But in plasma are substances which are vital to life : food chemicals, various salts, chemicals called *hormones* which are secreted by special glands and control growth and the development and action of the sex organs..

Certainly the most important substances found in blood plasma are complicated chemical compounds called anti-bodies.

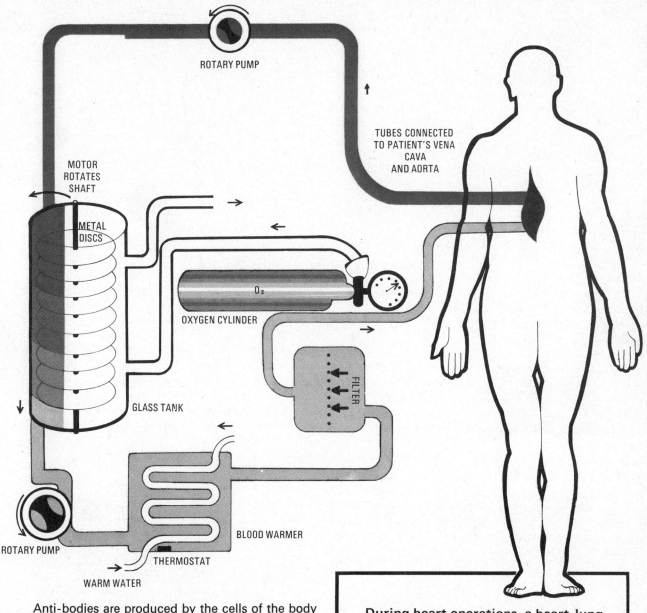

ROTARY PUMP

TUBES CONNECTED
TO PATIENT'S VENA
CAVA
AND AORTA

MOTOR
ROTATES
SHAFT

METAL
DISCS

O₂

OXYGEN CYLINDER

GLASS TANK

FILTER

ROTARY PUMP

BLOOD WARMER

THERMOSTAT

WARM WATER

Anti-bodies are produced by the cells of the body as a defence against disease. During normal life the body is constantly in contact with germs which could cause some particular illness, but gradually the body becomes immune against these germs because of the store-house of anti-bodies which gradually build up in the blood.

If, however, a person is planning to visit some country where he is liable to come into contact with germs of diseases like typhus and cholera, then he can be given special injections which can help his body quickly form the anti-bodies necessary to fight these diseases.

There are also anti-bodies in the blood which fight against cells which do not belong to the body, particularly the cells of some other person's heart or kidney which has been used in one or another of the now familiar transplant operations.

Doctors explain the fight anti-bodies wage against the new heart as tissue rejection. A great deal of medical research is now going on to discover ways in which the body can be made to accept rather than reject the particular organ which could keep the body alive.

During heart operations, a heart-lung machine can continue pumping blood through the body and supply it with oxygen, as this diagram shows. In the big glass tank, a series of rotating metal discs dipping into the blood bring it into contact with oxygen from the cylinder. Notice the coil of piping which keeps the blood at the normal temperature of the body.

The plasma also contains small saucer-shaped cells called *thrombocytes,* which are smaller than red cells. These cells cause a network of tiny crystals to form a clot and so prevent bleeding from a wound. Sometimes clots form without a noticeable injury, causing an illness called *thrombosis.* This can be very dangerous if medical help is not immediately given, as the clot can be carried along the blood stream and reach the heart, and perhaps cause a fatal heart attack.

39

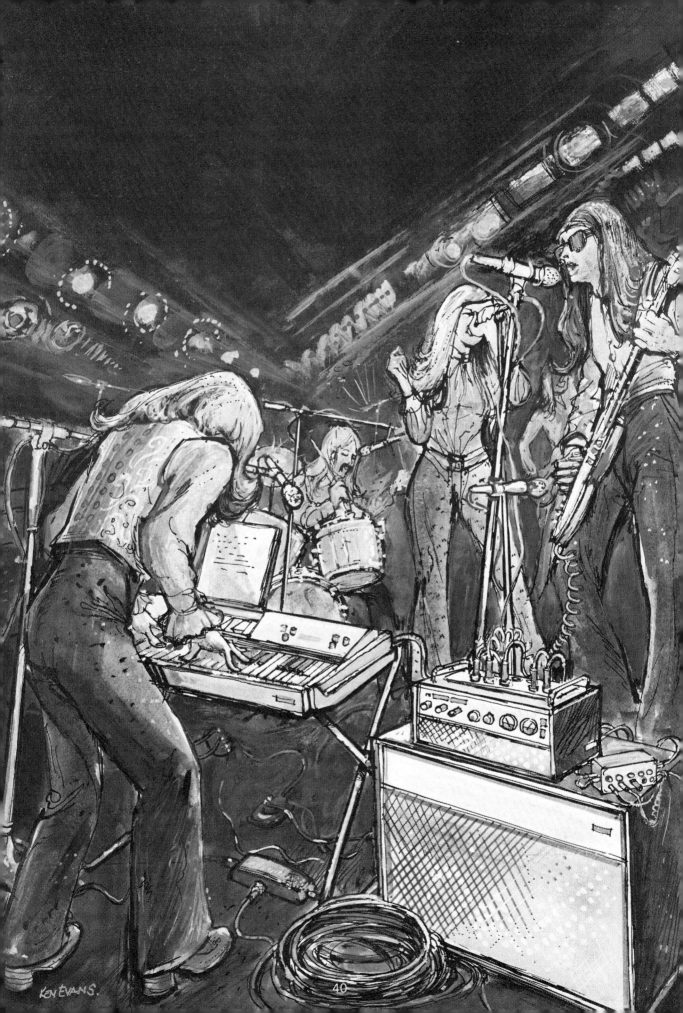

Today jazz, pop, and even classical musicians are depending more and more on developments in science and electronics to create new kinds of music.

SCIENCE GOES 'POP'

The beautiful Sitar, a type of Indian guitar.

USING scientific ideas for music-making is not completely new. More than 3,000 years ago Chinese musicians tried to relate the notes they played on their instruments to various colours, their own moods, and the seasons.

One of their instruments, called the *Ch'in*, was a type of zither or harp using silk strings. They attempted to work out a mathematical relationship between the strings by insisting that each string be made from a certain number of twisted strands of silk. The note played on each string was supposed to make one 'feel' a certain colour, and the wooden support or 'bridge' underneath that particular string was also painted in that particular colour.

About 2,000 years ago musicians in India went very deeply into the science and mathematics of music. They invented a scale dividing the *octave* (which today has eight notes) into no less than 64 tones. They quickly found

their music too complicated, and reduced their tones to 22, which they still use today.

A number of pop and jazz groups are now using the Indian instrument called the *Sitar*, a beautifully decorated long-necked type of guitar. Its strings 'buzz' slightly when they are plucked and give out a rather 'eastern' sound which has a surprising resemblance to some of the tones which musicians can get from electric guitars.

SCIENTIFIC

The Indians were probably the first to divide up a string into different lengths so that a scale could be played. Today every guitar player is totally dependent on this ancient piece of scientific research as the fingers on his left hand press the guitar strings down on the proper frets on the finger-board.

Not so long ago guitar players

would ask for an 'E', or 'A' or some other steel string in a music shop. Today, more and more musicians will ask for a '16 thou', a '9 thou' or some other gauge or thickness, rather than a musical note. Most steel guitar strings are scientifically graded in gauges quoted in thousandths of an inch, something the Chinese tried to do with silk, in effect, back in ancient times.

In the early 1930s very few musicians had even heard, let alone played, an electric-guitar.

Quite a number of guitar players, however, wanting to compete in volume with other musicians in the traditional 'big bands' of that jazz era, attached small microphones to their instruments. The microphones were connected to amplifiers and loudspeakers. The players not only found that their instruments played more loudly. The sound coming from their loudspeakers seemed to have a different quality. Something approaching the

41

A

CHOOSE YOUR SOUND . . .

Electronics has given a new meaning to music, with the "instruments" shown here.
A. Woodwind. This device imitates the sounds of an oboe, English horn and many other instruments.
B. Ring modulator. Guitar, electric organ or a singing voice channelled via an amplifier through this can be raised or lowered in pitch, superimposed on to each other or varied in volume. C. Percussion. Bongos, snare, tambourine and clave are among the sounds made by this machine.

B

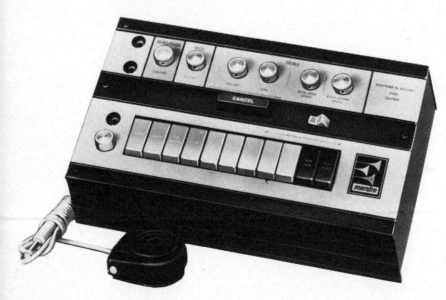

C

sound of the modern 'all-electric' guitar. Many players liked what they heard and began to think of the possibilities of using electronics in music seriously.

At about the same time the new electronic 'Hammond' organs were being designed and built. These instruments did not just make traditional pipe or reed organs sound louder using amplifiers and loudspeakers. They actually *created* sounds electronically.

A long rotating shaft inside the instrument had a number of toothed metal wheels attached to it, one for each note of the scale to be played on the organ's keyboard or manual. Each wheel rotated near a small electromagnet, which generated electrical currents vibrating at different rates or frequencies. These currents then were amplified to work a battery of loudspeakers.

NEW SOUNDS

The organ notes could be made to imitate the sounds of flutes, violins, oboes, and other instruments simply by using control switches which mixed together the basic notes coming from each rotating wheel. Inventive musicians quickly found that by using a little ingenuity they could adjust the switches to make 'new sounds' which had never been heard before.

Today, electronic organs are widely used by pop musicians. They are the same, in principle, as the first organs, but they are much smaller and more portable. Instead of heavy metal shafts and toothed

Science adds magic to the pop singer's songs.

wheels, they use compact transistorized units or oscillators to generate the basic notes of the scale. Most pop organ players rarely imitate traditional instruments: they adjust the proper electronic controls to make their own 'sounds.'

In the meantime the old 'amplified' guitar was becoming a new instrument in its own right. Each steel string had a small electromagnet placed near it. The string, when plucked, generated an electric current directly in the electromagnet. This was then amplified to work loudspeakers. Today electric-guitars do not even have to be made of thin wood to radiate sound. This is now done by the loudspeakers.

Modern electric-guitar players are highly skilled musicians who can 'coax' surprisingly original tone-colours and harmonies from their instruments.

In addition to the powerful amplifiers which make their instruments work, they use other types of electronic equipment to give extra 'dimensions' to their music. The music can be made to sound as if it were coming from a huge cavern by using echo units. Some of these are modified tape-recorders, in which the sound is continuously recorded on a tape 'loop', being played back again into the amplifiers a fraction of a second after the main sound has been played.

'LIGHT SHOWS'

Other electronic devices can imitate the *tremolo* of a pipe organ and the *vibrato* a singer or violin player uses.

More and more musicians are learning a great deal about electronics and are able to make additional equipment for their instruments in their search for newer and still newer 'sounds'. Yet another 'dimension' is being added to the sound using 'light shows'. Special lights of different colours keep flashing as the music is played. Some light shows are incredibly complex electronically: the lights are connected to the amplifiers of the instruments in such a way that they can flash and change colour in time with the rhythm of the group.

Certainly, the most ingenious (and complicated) addition to a musician's range of equipment is the now famous moog synthesizer, invented about ten years ago by a Danish electronic engineer whose name was Moog (pronounced Moge).

This instrument, which has been used by the BBC for making unusual types of music and sound effects, can create almost any type of sound. It can also make amazing changes in the tones of traditional instruments. When played through the moog synthesizer a Spanish guitar can sound like a church organ or a bagpipe, a violin can resemble the human voice or the song of a bird, and a piano can rival the space-age thunder of a Saturn-5 moon-rocket at blast-off!

Until recently our knowledge of the universe has been limited to those regions of outer space which could be studied with optical telescopes and photographic film. Today an entirely new universe is being revealed by radio receivers, geiger counters and satellites in orbit.

THE UNSEEN UNIVERSE

THE "new astronomy", as it is often called, began almost by accident back in 1932. Karl Jansky, an American electronics engineer, was studying the interference or "static" that kept spoiling the reception of most short wave radio receptions of that time.

Jansky noticed that a strange hissing noise was always heard from his radio receiver whenever the radio's aerial was pointed up at a certain region of the sky, particularly from the group of stars making up the constellation of Sagittarius. Jansky finally concluded that he must be hearing signals from outer space.

Although many astronomers did not seem to be interested in this discovery, a radio amateur certainly was. He was Grote Reber, also an American, and he quickly built himself a relatively crude radio telescope, using lengths of wood, some old motor car parts, and a radio set Reber had been using for short wave reception.

Within a few weeks Reber was listening in to signals definitely coming from several constellations. He also heard strong signals coming from the Sun.

Then, during World War Two, the new science of radio astronomy really began in earnest, particularly when it was noticed that the Sun was quite obviously having an effect on radar equipment.

Since those early beginnings radio telescopes have quickly become widely used by astronomers as the traditional "light" telescopes. The big radar "dishes" of the war have been transformed and modified to make the giant telescopes at Jodrell Bank in England and at Parkes in Australia. In Puerto Rico a mountain valley has been used to make a giant 1,000 foot diameter "dish" to focus radio waves from outer space on to a tiny aerial suspended by cables from three steel pylons mounted on neighbouring hills.

Using these new instruments astronomers have discovered surprising facts about the universe.

Observations of the radio waves from the Sun have proved

Radio waves from outer space are measured and located by Britain's Jodrell Bank radio-telescope in Cheshire (above), which has also tracked both American and Russian space craft. The telescope (left), at Lord's Bridge observatory, is picking up radio waves from galaxies more than 8,000 million light years away.

American technicians check an astronomical observatory, of the kind that will be put into earth-orbit to make observations, freed from the distortions of the Earth's atmosphere.

that the Sun's "atmosphere" or *corona* is not just a relatively thin layer of electrified gas just above the Sun's visible surface. It extends millions of miles out into space. In fact the Earth and neighbouring planets are now known to be *inside* the Sun's corona.

One of the most important research jobs being done using radio telescopes is the investigation of the mysterious "quasi-stellar objects" or *quasars.*

At first these appeared to be very faint stars when observed with ordinary telescopes. Then they were found to be giving off very powerful radio waves. Now they are known to be some of the most distant objects discovered in the universe. So far away are they that their radio signals, travelling at 186,000 miles a second, have taken at least 8,000 million years to reach our radio telescopes. And they are also believed to be incredibly large, probably as much as 50 million million miles in diameter.

It is still not definitely known what quasars are and why they are able to give off such enormous amounts of energy, considering how far away they are.

One fascinating theory is that quasars are objects which have become so dense, possibly a million times denser than lead, that they are collapsing or imploding under the titanic force of their own gravity. Of course we cannot know exactly what is happening to them *now*, because what we observe now took place 8,000 million years ago. In effect radio telescopes allow us to listen-in to the distant past.

Radio astronomers are also mystified by the *pulsars:* very small objects within our own galaxy which give off a quick burst of radio energy every second or so. They are believed to be enormously heavy spheres about 10 miles across, with a 100 mile long "bar" of radio-activity running through them. They are also thought to be spinning around, and we receive the radio "pulse" every time the "bar" is at a certain angle to our Earth.

MYSTERY OBJECTS

On January 31, 1958, America launched her first satellite into orbit around the Earth. Called Explorer 1, this satellite carried instruments similar to geiger counters which could detect and measure the strengths of radioactive particles.

As it swept high in orbit around the Earth the satellite detected the existence of something which came as an almost complete surprise to most scientists and astronomers.

From subsequent observations made with later satellites we know now that the Earth is surrounded by two enormous doughnut-shaped regions of radioactivity, extending more than 10,000 miles out into space. Called the Van Allen Belts after the scientist who used many satellite observations to plot their sizes and shapes, they were formed when tiny particles of radiation from the Sun became "trapped" by the magnetic field of force surrounding the Earth.

Satellites are becoming more and more useful to the astronomer. In the past astronomers were hampered by the fact that the atmosphere weakened or blocked off radiation from outer space.

Satellites, however, can rise above the atmosphere and carry special instruments which can measure all kinds of radiation: ultra-violet rays, streams of atomic particles, X-rays, and cosmic rays which are tiny particles moving at speeds approaching the speed of light, most of them coming from mysterious regions far beyond the solar system.

Neutrinos (a word which means "the little neutral ones") are atomic particles many scientists claim cannot really exist. They are so fantastically tiny that in calculations scientists are obliged to treat neutrinos as having zero mass. They are also electrically neutral, having neither a positive nor a negative electrical "charge".

Yet billions upon billions of neutrinos are believed to be reaching the Earth from all over the universe every second, and being so tiny they pass through everything, straight through the Earth, emerging from the other side of the Earth, and then continuing their journey through space. In spite of this, ways have been found of detecting neutrinos.

Deep down in a deserted mine shaft in South Africa an immense tank has been filled with 100,000 gallons of carbon tetrachloride, which is used normally as a cleaning fluid for clothes.

Suspended in the tank is a battery of hundreds of *scintillation counters*. These are instruments which give off tiny flashes of light when a small crystal is struck by certain kinds of atomic particles, including neutrinos.

It is hoped that this elaborate apparatus will be able to detect about *one* neutrino every week, which scientists consider quite a good catch!

Still more amazing things about the "unseen universe" may be discovered by these bizarre neutrino-telescopes in the future.

Above: the huge bowl aerial of a radio telescope at Arecibo, Puerto Rico. This has a diameter of 1,000 feet, and the dish covers 1½ acres.

Dr. James Van Allen, who discovered the regions of radio-activity around the Earth, known as the Van Allen Belts.

SCIENCE QUIZ

Now you have read the Science section of this book, see how many of the questions you can answer in the quiz below. All the answers are at the back of the book.

1 The study of forests, oceans, the atmosphere and other parts of the Earth's environment in relation to life inhabiting the earth has a particular name. Do you know what it is?

2 What happened to much of Krakatoa island in 1883, and how has its environment changed since?

3 The average family fills one dustbin a week with rubbish. How many dustbins may they fill in ten years' time?

4 Karl Jansky heard a strange hissing on his radio receiver and came to a conclusion that the signals came from an unexpected source. What was this source?

5 These experiments were followed by Grote Reber who heard signals from various constellations. But what gave him the strongest signal?

6 What is another name for the sun's atmosphere?

7 The earth is surrounded by two enormous doughnut-shaped regions of radio activity, extending more than 10,000 miles out in space. What are these called?

8 A musical instrument used by the Chinese was a kind of zither or harp which used silk strings. What was this called? What were the notes supposed to make one feel?

9 When Indian musicians went deeply into the science and mathematics of music, they divided the octave into a certain number of tones. Do you know how many they chose? When they found this made their music too complicated, to how many tones did they reduce the octave?

10 What instrument, used sometimes by pop groups, comes from India and is a beautifully decorated, long-necked type of guitar which makes a rather "eastern" sound?

11 Do you know to which nation belonged the people who were the first to divide a string into different lengths so that a scale could be played?

12 When guitar players wanted to compete in volume with other musicians in the big bands of the jazz era, what did they attach to their instruments?

13 In the early electronic organs, toothed metal wheels rotated near electro-magnets. What did these generate and what was the end result?

14 A Danish engineer invented a device which can create almost any type of sound and change the sound of traditional instruments. What is this called?

15 What factor gave a tremendous impetus to methods of transport in Britain and made the current vehicles appear slow and outmoded?

16 What were the three inventions which enabled man to increase the efficiency of ships, before the introduction of steam?

17 After the introduction of steamships, a voyage from Britain to India took only six weeks. What event in 1896 made this possible?

18 How long did a similar journey take in 1800?

19 Name the two kinds of ships' engines used after oil had replaced coal as a fuel.

20 What significant milestone in water transport was passed in 1959?

21 How did a French inventor, Clement Ader, make history in 1890 in a steam-driven machine?

22 Who made the first true powered, sustained and controlled flights in a 12 h.p. engined biplane in 1903?

23 In what year was the sound barrier broken by an American jet plane, Bell X5-1?

24 Who made history as the first man in orbit around the earth, and when did Apollo II land on the moon?

25 Who first discovered how blood circulates?

26 Nine million blood cells are created, and others destroyed, in the body in a certain length of time. How long does this process take?

27 Do you know what erythocytes are?

28 Can you say how much blood passes through the heart in one day?

29 Blood is divided into groups known as A, B and O. When was this classification first arrived at?

ARCTIC TRAWLER

A huge mountain of water towered menacingly over a fishing trawler steaming northwards to the Arctic fishing grounds. For an instant, the wave hovered, then it crashed down, swinging the trawler high on its crest.

"Red Charger" was lucky. Few ships emerge without damage from their encounter with an Arctic storm. Most are badly battered, with deck fittings ripped away. Men can be swept into the water so cold that it can stop the heart in five minutes.

Even if they survive the intense cold by some miracle, there are the deadly killer whale and mighty Greenland shark waiting to finish off the job.

Yet, despite the dangers, there is a down-to-earth heartiness among the crews that is characteristic of their hard-working shipboard lives. George Goldsmith Carter found this when he put to sea in "Red Charger" and wrote about it in his book of the same name.

"Red Charger's" destination was the haddock grounds of Andenes on the north-west coast of Norway. On her journey, she would encounter the Wall of Death. In reality, this is the continental shelf of the north-west coast of Norway where a ship can

The duties of the fishermen are arduous and often monotonous. They welcome the chance to share a hot drink and swop yarns about their lives on shore and at sea.

sail into dangerously shallow water from several hundred fathoms very quickly.

Here, deep currents flowing on to the steep, hidden mountain under the ocean, drive surface-wards like a rushing torrent and turn the sea into a boiling turmoil. Ships can be driven on to hidden rocks or sucked into crevasses by the currents.

The wall of death . . . an apt name! Fifteen ships from Fleetwood alone perished here in ten to twelve years, and most of them with all hands. Many more wrecks from which the crews, or some of them, had been rescued litter this fisherman's graveyard.

Carter was once at the offices of a trawler company when one of its vessels was overdue. A group of haggard-eyed women, who grew more hopeless each day, waited at the office doors for news of their missing husbands or sons.

Theirs was the tragedy of those who can only wait and hope. At sea, in the face of driving winds from the north, all fears are swamped by the tremendous activity of fishing and gutting, working and sleeping, eating and swapping yarns.

From Aberdeen, Granton, North Shields, Hull, Grimsby, Lowestoft, Milford Haven and Fleetwood sail the men who fish in distant waters, mainly in the North Atlantic.

They are after cod and haddock, sole and plaice, herring and whiting and hake. Carter set sail from Fleetwood in a trawler one hundred and forty feet long with a beam of twenty-four feet, which arrived at its fishing grounds in five days.

These were not far from the Lofoten Islands and the maelstrom, where the tides beat against each other and form whirlpools like pits in the ocean. Men and boats have been drawn into these dreadful voids.

"Red Charger" began fishing in one hundred and twenty fathoms. The net, a vast assembly of bobbins and floats and an intricate tracery of twine, was launched behind the ship and dragged over the sea bed. Paravanes kept open the mouth, shaped like a "D" lying on its back.

As the trawler ploughed on under the tremendous weight of the tackle it was dragging through the ocean, men began preparing the fish pounds. These are places on the deck where the fish are de-gutted and beheaded.

Working at speed, the men grab a big cod by the gills, rip out the liver and toss it into a nearby basket. This is boiled for the oil. The intestines, roe and chitterlings are tossed overboard to the hovering gulls and other birds.

The rattling of the winch meant that the net was being hauled in with its catch of two hundred and fifty stone of haddocks from the icy depths of the Norwegian haddock grounds. To bring the net in took twenty-eight minutes. It was emptied into the pounds and the slashing and gutting began.

"Once you have been on the Arctic fishing grounds and have seen the men at work, it is easy to understand why British fishermen are the toughest and most skilful in the world," says Carter. They can be nothing else, he says, among the blasting cold and black terror and discomfort of the Arctic Seas.

A change of position followed and a journey of fifty-five miles brought "Red Charger" to the edge of the Wall of Death. The net was lowered and was brought back to the surface tightly packed with haddock, cod and coal fish. It went back into the sea and returned to the surface again and again until the pounds were swimming with fish and the men were working like demons with their flashing knives.

Soon, the men's eyes were red with fatigue. They had worked unceasingly for long hours. All the time, the wind grew stronger and the seas rougher. "Red Charger" tossed and rolled her rails under the ocean, while the men went on working the net, which chafed their wrists into rings of vicious sea boils, or chopped and slashed with their knives in the pounds.

The ship was filled with the sickly smell of cods' livers being boiled to oil in the stern. When it was finished, the waste matter was shot overboard with a blast of steam, to the delight of the always-hungry sea birds.

Cups of tea, tots of rum and yarns about service in other ships and experiences on shore, keep the men's spirits up during their arduous and sometimes monotonous duties.

But there is no flagging until the ship is on its way home again with its catch of haddock, whiting and cod for the fish shops. The snow and ice on its deck and lines will slowly melt as it leaves the frozen Arctic waters and heads for home.

In time, port is sighted. The ship passes through the lock gates where shore hands wait to unload the vessel.

After a few days at home, the men will be off to sea again . . . back to the tough life they always grumble about, but really enjoy.

Home at last and the catch is unloaded. The fish will be sold and distributed to towns and villages all over the country. For the fisherman there is the chance to spend some time with his family—and then it's off to sea again.

Like lonely, lovely jewels in the sunny Indian ocean are the Seychelles Islands, where pirates once hid their treasure and where a disguised slave trader began a strange panic.

SECRET OF THE SEYCHELLES

MEN working in the fields of one of the sunny Seychelles islands in the Indian ocean looked up in surprise when a lookout shouted a sharp warning. "There's a British ship in the harbour," he cried.

Pierre Poivre, the island's French governor, joined the lookout on his high vantage point and confirmed the identity of the new arrival, a four-masted sailing barque.

Resignedly he shrugged his shoulders. "The British will discover our secret, unless we act quickly," he mused.

Then he gave a startling order. "Set fire to the crops," he cried. "Quickly! There is no time to waste. The British sailors must not discover what we are growing here."

In amazement, the men obeyed his order. Before long, the crops they had been carefully tending were crackling with fire in the warmth of the sun. And in a little while, fanned by the wind, the flames had transformed the plants into unidentifiable ash.

Poivre was satisfied, but he was to regret his hasty action. The plants that were so impetuously burnt were of various spices, which

were then a valuable luxury in Europe. Because the Dutch had the monopoly of the spice trade, which they grew on their possessions and sold to the world at whatever prices they could command, Poivre had sought to break the Dutch domination and create profits for his own country.

Realising that the Seychelles archipelago was free from hurricanes, he had spice plantations planted there in secret. He wanted nobody to know what he was doing, not even the British who could possibly intrude upon the

trade themselves and so bring down the prices and cause him to lose profits.

By setting fire to his plantations, he hoped to keep his secret, and perhaps create his plantations afresh when there were no suspicious ships in the harbour.

But, when he went down to the harbour to investigate the barque, Poivre had a shock. True, there was hostility from the captain and crew when he first went aboard. However, as soon as Poivre and the captain realised that they were both fellow countrymen, their greeting was friendly.

In some bewilderment, Poivre asked, "Why are you showing the British flag if you are a French ship."

The captain gave Poivre a sly look and, with a rueful laugh, took him down to the hold. Packed tightly in the confined space were scores of sweating brown bodies, many weak from lack of food, gasping for life in an indescribable stench.

"Slaves," exclaimed Poivre. "You are a French slave ship."

"Now you know why I flew the British flag," said the captain. "I thought this island was occupied by the British. I didn't want my

masts shot away."

Poivre stumped angrily off the ship. He had destroyed his crop for nothing. The "British" ship was French, and a slaver at that.

All this happened in 1778, when there had been a French settlement on these islands for ten years, although they had been annexed for France in 1744.

The early explorer who claimed the 92 islands of the Syechelles with an area of 156 square miles was a French sea captain named Lazarre Picault, who landed there in 1742 and returned again two years later to take possession of them.

To the largest island he gave the name of Mahé, in honour of the governor of Mauritius, Mahé de Labourdonnais. In 1756, the whole group was renamed out of respect to Vicomte Moreau des Séchelles, a minister of Louis the Fifteenth.

A squadron of British ships captured the islands in 1774, although the British did not occupy them for twenty years. De Quinssy, the French commander, remained in control, raising the French tricolour when French ships approached, and another flag bearing the words "Seychelles Capitulation" when the British came.

All the successive invaders were captivated by the beauty of the Seychelles and their pleasant climate which creates an abundance of flowering plants. One who fell in love with them was Colonel Charles Gordon, later made famous at Khartoum in

Africa where he was besieged and killed in 1885 by rebels.

Gordon went to Mauritius in 1881 as Commanding Royal Engineer. Mauritius is also in the Indian ocean, and so it was natural that he should visit the Seychelles, a dependency of Mauritius since 1810.

To him, they were beautiful islands, and he declared that he had found the site of paradise, a place of perfect delight, in the Vallée de Mai on Praslin. He also believed that the Seychelles were part of a continent submerged by the flood from which Noah escaped in his ark in the Bible.

When they were first visited by Europeans, the Seychelles were uninhabited. Mauritian and Bour-

bon creoles later colonised the islands, being joined subsequently by French and British people. Freed slaves from East Africa made their homes there and, with the passing of the years, there grew up a cosmopolitan population which included Chinese and Indian arrivals.

Britain seized the islands from France in 1810 and they were ceded to Britain by the Treaty of Paris in 1814. Until 1903, the Seychelles and Mauritius were administered as a single colony.

Victoria in Mahé Island is the capital and it has a curious link with London. This is a cast-iron clock tower which is a replica of Big Ben and provides a local term for any simpleton or country

A Seychelles blacksmith works at his craft (far left) on the island of La Digue. Fish traps, like that being woven on the left, are used extensively by fishermen who sink them beneath the water (right) to catch their unwary victims.

bumpkin—"He hasn't seen the clock."

Whether the people live in Victoria, whose houses are built of coral hewn into building blocks which glistens like marble from a distance, in hamlets along the sea shore, or in estates on the hills, they are happy in their sunny and peaceful haven in the Indian ocean.

Their lives are the contented ones of people close to nature, whose livelihoods come from the sea and the land. Coconuts, cinnamon and vanilla are grown here. The last two are exported to bring money to the islands, and from the coconuts are made copra (the dried kernels of the coconut which can be made into margarine, candles, medicine, ointments and soap, especially a marine soap which lathers in salt water) and coconut oil.

Guano is another export. It consists of the droppings of land and sea birds, which are sent to buyers overseas who process it in their factories to extract the phosphorus, which is used in the manufacture of matches, in vermin killers and for other purposes. Also obtained from guano is ammonia, a valuable ingredient of fertilisers, medicines, dyes and explosives. This is used, too, in refrigerating plants.

Most of the islands are of granite, fringed by coral reefs in places, and the most famous fruit which grows on them is the Maldive double coconut, or *coco de mer*.

Although the only mammals are the rat and the bat, there are lizards and snakes. But the real life among the trees and rocky inlets is provided by the variety of birds, including terns, gannets and white egrets.

Although their exports make such valuable contributions to the outside world, the people of the Seychelles live much as they have done for hundreds of years.

But for all its old world beauty, the Seychelles cannot avoid the present. On Mahé, the Americans have set up a satellite tracking station, and the progress of futuristic space craft orbiting the world is tracked in this distant archipelago in the Indian Ocean.

Visitors arrive on Praslin island (left). The main island of Mahé lies in the background. On this there is a satellite tracking station, to which the seaplane (right) is bringing supplies.

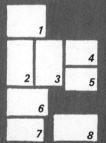

1. Austria, 3s. 2. Japan, 10 yen. 3. Japan, 8 yen. 4. Japan, 40 yen. 5. Japan, 5.00 yen. 6. Belgium, 6F. 7. Uruguay, 10c. 8. Monaco, c50. 9. Hungary, 60f. 10. Hungary, 20f. 11. Tanzania, 5c. 12. Canada, 5 cents. 13. Rhodesia and Nyasaland, 1/-. 14. Southern Rhodesia, 2d.

RLD
ATER

by C. W. Hill

WATER, water everywhere, nor any drop to drink!" cried the Ancient Mariner in Samuel Coleridge's poem of that name. His ship was becalmed on a tropical sea and, although they were surrounded by water, the sailors were dying of thirst.

About 97% of the world's water consists of salt sea and two-thirds of the other 3% is permanently frozen, either in the polar regions or as glaciers in high mountain ranges. Mankind depends for survival on the remaining 1%.

During the ten years ending in 1974 the countries of Unesco (United Nations Educational, Scientific and Cultural Organisation), have been co-operating to study ways of protecting water resources. To commemorate the International Hydrological Decade, Canada has issued a special 5-cents stamp whose design illustrates the cycle of water on earth. This begins with rain falling either into the sea or on land, where it forms lakes and rivers flowing into the sea. Here it evaporates to form clouds which in turn provide the rain to begin the cycle again.

All the stages in this cycle, as well as the extra steps introduced by man in the form of artificial lakes, dams and canals, can be illustrated in a stamp collection. Rain is falling on a large Japanese 10-yen stamp which reproduces an old print entitled "Lady returning from the bath-house". Another Japanese stamp, issued in 1958 to mark International Letter-writing Week, has a fine picture of a stormy sea.

Many countries have issued stamps with views of waterfalls. The most spectacular in Africa are the Victoria Falls on the Zambesi River. They were named in 1855 by the explorer David Livingstone, the first European to see them, and they have been featured on several Rhodesian stamps. Niagara Falls and the Kaieteur Falls, in Guyana, which are five times the height of Niagara, have also appeared on attractive pictorials.

Waterfalls can be harnessed to provide power for turbines which generate electricity, but in places where no suitable natural falls exist, artificial waterfalls can be created by building dams. The water held back by a dam may also be used for irrigating arid land or to control the flow of a river liable to serious flooding.

The nationalisation of Austria's electricity industry was commemorated by a series of stamps showing dams and hydro-electric power stations, among them the Grossraming Dam on the River Enns. The Kariba Dam, on the Zambesi, the Shannon Barrage, in Ireland, and the Shihmen Dam, in Taiwan, are among other dams for which special stamps have been issued. Hydroelectric power is also featured on many issues, including a 5-cents stamp from Tanzania and an 8-fen stamp from China, showing a turbo-generator being installed at the Hsinankiang power station.

One of the first men to make a scientific study of the sea was Prince Albert of Monaco. He is portrayed on a 50-centimes stamp issued in Monaco in 1960 to celebrate the fiftieth anniversary of the opening of his Oceanographic Museum. His portrait is flanked by two yachts, *Hirondelle I* and *Princesse Alice*, in which the Prince made long voyages to pursue his researches.

Because they are flat countries, Belgium and Holland have an important network of ship canals. A view of the Belgian canal port of Zandvliet, claimed to be the largest in the world, forms the design of a recent Belgian 6-francs stamp and several series have been devoted to Dutch canals.

A "Water on Stamps" collection would not be complete without a selection of stamps featuring water sports. Even land-locked Hungary can offer the pleasures of swimming and canoeing on Lake Balaton, the largest lake in central Europe.

THE ARABIAN NIGHTS RAILWAY

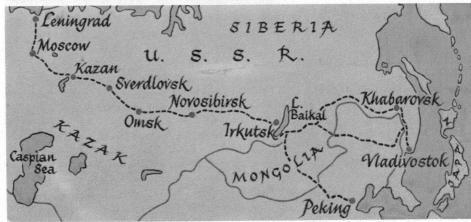

Tsar Alexander III (left) ordered the building of the railway, whose route is shown on the map above. At first, accidents were frequent (below) and passengers were forced to trudge many miles through snow to the nearest village. They were caused because the track was light and badly laid.

TSAR Alexander III of Russia shuffled through the official papers on his desk without much interest. It was unlikely that among them he would find the solution to a problem that was giving him many sleepless nights.

'More and more Chinese are crossing the border into Russia every day,' he said musingly to the secretary who stood at his side. 'We should move troops to the border to keep a tight reign on this illegal immigration.'

'But the border is thousands of miles away,' protested his secretary, a civil servant of long experience. 'The journey takes many weeks and the conditions through Siberia are intolerable.'

'True,' agreed the Tsar. He tossed the papers aside. Then, suddenly, he jabbed his finger on a report that his ceaseless shuffling had brought to the surface. 'There's our answer,' he cried. 'A plan for a railway line from St. Petersburg to Vladivostok and Port Arthur. We will enquire into this.'

Enquire into it, he did. Committees were appointed to examine the plan, and they were finally stirred into action by the news that engineers were considering building a rival line in China.

'It is essential to proceed with

Sidings were added to the line in 1899, when a regular train service had begun. But the 7,000 goods wagons in use caused constant blockages (above). In the winter, the lines were laid across frozen Lake Baikal (below).

the construction of this line,' ordered the Tsar. His son, the Tsarevitch Nicholas, filled a wheelbarrow with clay at the grand opening, using a ceremonial shovel, and emptied it upon an embankment.

It was 31st May, 1891, and work had at last begun on the most fantastic railway in the world, the Trans-Siberian. Built almost entirely by unskilled labour that included Chinese coolies and the inmates of Siberian prison camps, this 4,950 mile long rail link between the Ural mountains and Vladivostok was the big joke of the engineering world.

'You had better let us help you,' the top railway experts of the West had said to the Russian authorities 'After all, we understand how railways are built.'

The Russians said politely that they thought they could manage the job themselves. Only the fact that they knew virtually nothing about railways enabled them to go ahead and tackle a job that many engineers would have thought was impossible.

With unskilled labour, they started to put down a track of such poor quality that people said that it would not support a single cattle truck, let alone a full-sized train.

Yet, when it was opened, it worked, and went on working. It was—and still is—the longest continuous railway line on earth.

To keep down construction costs, it was decided to avoid tunnelling and hill cutting, if these merely reduced curves and gradients for greater safety. Timber was subsituted for steel whereever possible, and steam ferries saved the cost of long-span metal bridges.

Probably, the most unusual feature of the whole undertaking was the cheerful disregard for places. If the straightest and easiest route between two points meant missing a large town by several miles, then that was just unfortunate for travellers to that particular place.

They descended at the appropriate station and it was not until they had left the platform that they discovered that there was nothing to be seen but miles of snow. Years later, extension lines were constructed, but for a while local cab drivers did a roaring trade.

The sheer labour involved in spanning thousands of miles of inhospitable country in all weathers was incredible.

In summer, as they crossed the Steppes, the men hacked their way through jungles of stinging nettles eight feet tall, felling acres of timber and filling up innumerable small lakes, through a haze of gnats and mosquitoes that tortured them beyond endurance.

In winter, bridge builders would fall to their deaths as they grew clumsy in sub-zero temperatures. To keep the supplies of raw materials moving, the contractors thought nothing of driving freight trains across frozen rivers, with the tracks frozen direct to the ice.

With serviceable track growing

from both the western and eastern terminals, considerable portions of the railway were in use before the two ends were joined. But, at last there was an uninterrupted permanent way from the Urals to Vladivostok.

In those days, nobody could pretend that the Trans-Siberian railway was fast, for the poor quality of the rails made it impossible to exceed 20 miles an hour. Snow drifted across the tracks in winter, and the train was constantly being held up while men were found to dig it out.

Fuel and water supplies were so far apart that the boilers often ran dry before the next water tower could be reached, and wooden bridges were regularly burnt down because of the crews' habit of carelessly showering them with red hot cinders.

There was one even more pressing problem. There were no restaurant cars and, in theory, everyone ate when the train reached a station. At a big station, food was plentiful and cheap. A visitor in 1898 recorded having 'soup, as fine a beefsteak as I ever ate, a splendid roast chicken, potatoes, vegetables and a bottle of beer for one rouble—about two shillings.'

But at most stations, one bought black bread and hard-boiled eggs from a local woman or—as often happened—went hungry.

The end of the 19th century very nearly saw the end of the Trans-Siberian railway as well. Short of money, men and equipment, it was staggering towards

Traffic was suspended for days in 1915 when a terrible fire broke out in the Siberian forests, caused by bonfires of dry grass-cuttings lit by foresters.

such complete chaos that the Tsar had to authorise a grant of several million pounds to avert a catastrophe. Then, rather as though they had grown tired of the world joking about their 'white elephant', the Russians made an enormous effort, and turned their 5,000 mile long nightmare into one of the mechanical wonders of the world.

It was the arrival of the luxury trains that worked the miracle, the unbelievable, legendary State Express. Each of these trains consisted of a high speed locomotive, to which was attached a baggage and service car.

Then followed a restaurant, and then a lounge car complete with piano, easy chairs, writing tables and a library stocked with books in many languages.

There were luxurious sleeping coaches with wall to wall carpeting as well as a complete church on wheels ministered over by a resident priest, and with a pair of bells mounted above the roof.

In case passengers felt in need of exercise during the ten day journey from Moscow to Vladivostok, there was a fully-equipped gymnasium with stationary bicycles and superb showers.

This incredible train linked up with European expresses, so that it was quite possible to board a train in London and travel straight through to Vladivostok—a journey that took 16 days and cost £32. Quite rightly, it became the ultimate in travel experiences.

It was all too good to last. World War One, followed by World War Two, put an end to the Arabian Nights railway. The journey can still be made, and the rolling stock is luxurious and impressive, running punctually behind its high speed diesel and electric locomotives.

But somehow, the magic has gone and today's "Rocket Express" just adds up to a slightly ordinary train. The State Express with its library, church and gymnasium have all passed into history.

The line ends at Vladivostok, Russia's main Pacific port, where the harbour is kept open by ice-breakers all the year round.

FORTUNE HUNTERS OF THE OUTBACK

Thousands of Australians threw up their jobs and trekked across the Blue Mountains to make their fortunes. All of them were in search of the same thing — gold

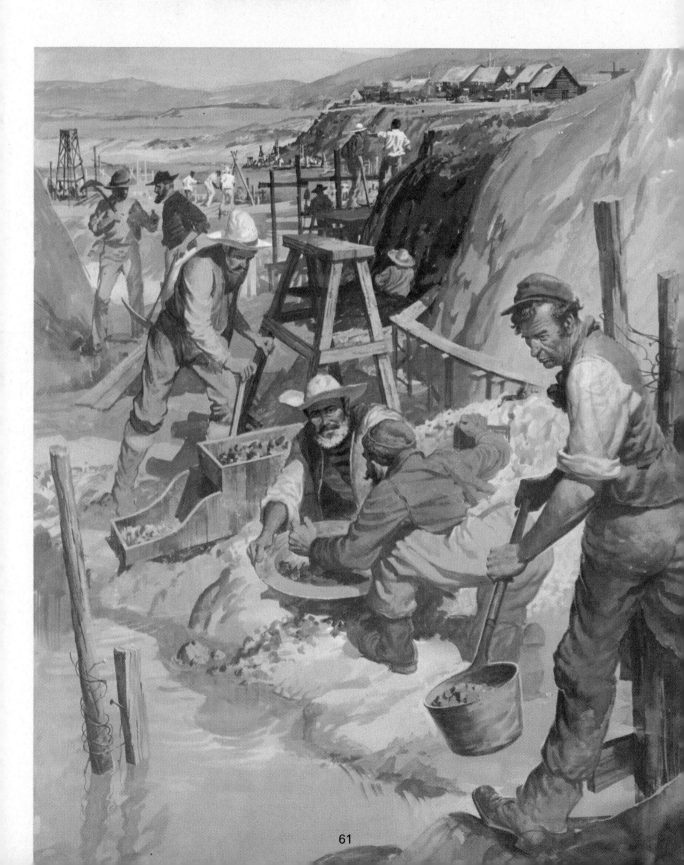

Young and old alike are fascinated by the possibility of finding gold glittering among the gravel.

EDWARD Hammond Hargraves saw a water hole in an Australian creek bed and said to a friend beside him, "We are now walking over a goldfield."

Scarcely believing him, his friend, John Lister, shovelled some gravel into a pan and washed it in the creek. Immediately, they found traces of gold.

This was no surprise to Hargraves, a veteran of the Californian gold rush of 1849. He had been among the many Australians who made the voyage to America and it was he who was eventually to start the gold rush in Australia.

At the age of 33, attracted by stories of gold in the United States, he sailed for California. But before long, he said that he knew of similar country back in Australia. Hargraves announced his intention of going home and finding gold there.

Whether he could recognise gold-bearing areas by their geological formation, or had merely heard stories of gold finds, is not known. It was true that rumours were rife that gold was to be found in Australia. When two geologists found important deposits near Hartley, New South Wales in 1839 and 1841, they only reinforced a suspicion which had been going around for some time.

In fact, it had already been found, probably by James McBrien, a government surveyor, who had reported a find in the Fish River Valley, New South Wales, as early as 1823.

However, although all these three had found it, all of them had managed to keep it a secret—with the advice of the authorities, of course.

But then, two things happened which were to influence the course of events in Australia. In 1840, New South Wales ceased to be regarded as a penal colony and the number of free settlers began to outnumber the prisoners and freed convicts. And then, during the late 1840's, gold was discovered in California. More Australians than before were free to seek their fortunes in America, and other arrivals were able to come to Australia to search for gold there.

One of those who returned was Hargraves. When he reached Australia in 1851, he made straight for the country which bore a similarity to the Californian gold rush area. Hiring a horse at Sydney, he set out across the Blue Mountains and eventually arrived at a place called Guyong.

There he met Lister, a young man who had long been enthralled by tales of gold. Nothing could stop him from accompanying Hargraves, and in February, 1851, the two men set out for a place which Hargraves said would be rich in gold.

Although there had been reports of gold in the area before no one, apart from Hargraves, with his experiences in California, really understood how to produce it from the earth.

In particular, the method of washing for alluvial gold from the river sands was quite unknown in Australia. Before long, they found their water hole and their deposits of gold.

However, they did not make a great deal of money from their discoveries. They returned to Sydney, and

An old prospector pans for gold in the time-honoured way, like the gold rush veterans of a century ago.

Hargraves told the Government of his finds, asking only that they should give him £10,000 as a reward. The Government did as he asked, but also made him commissioner of the goldfields.

And, then the news was made widely known. Immediately, gold rush fever struck Australia, and thousands of fortune hunters made for the goldfields. Doctors, lawyers, bootblacks, butchers, bakers and others in their thousands threw up their jobs in the towns and joined in the long trek across the Blue Mountains.

That same year, gold was discovered in the Buninyong Ranges near Ballarat, and that was the start of the Victorian gold rush. This gold field proved immensely rich, for during the November of 1851 alone the gold carried by the Government escort from Ballarat to Melbourne weighed two-and-a-half tons, about a third of the total amount raised in the goldfields as a whole.

With the discovery of the goldfields, the population of Australia began to increase rapidly. From all over the world, excited prospectors arrived at the diggings.

As in California, there were many unfortunate stories to be told. One, in particular, was enacted in Victoria and elsewhere. Diggers were so badly treated by officialdom, especially the goldfield constables, that eventually they rose in revolt.

Originally, Sir George Gibbs, governor of New South Wales, had asked that the find should be kept quiet because he feared that the lust for gold would drive men to lawlessness and to such a revolt as this.

Fortunately, it was settled peacefully when the goldfield constables became more diplomatic.

It was a miner's dream to strike it rich, to find just one big nugget of gold which would bring a fortune. But even small nuggets turned out to be few and far between at first. But the gold seekers' imaginations were fired when the first big nugget was discovered in New South Wales in July, 1851.

Known as the Kerr Hundredweight, this was a block of quartz and gold weighing 2,400 ounces and containing 1,272 ounces of gold. (In troy weight, the system by which gold is measured, there are 1,200 ounces in a hundredweight.)

The Holtermann nugget, also found in New South Wales, was the largest ever discovered, weighing 7,560 ounces and containing about 3,000 ounces of gold. Probably the most famous nugget of all was the "Welcome Stranger" found near Ballarat in 1858. This was a lump of pure gold weighing well over 2,000 ounces and worth at the time about £7,000.

Today, Australia ranks fourth among the gold producing nations of the world. This is because gold has been discovered in other states of Australia, notably Queensland, and in Western Australia. Here, in the aptly-named "Golden Mile" reef between the towns of Kalgoorlie and Boulder are some of the richest gold mines in the world.

Australia now produces over 700,000 ounces of gold a year, and in the whole of the country, since gold mining first began, more than 186 million ounces of gold have been produced.

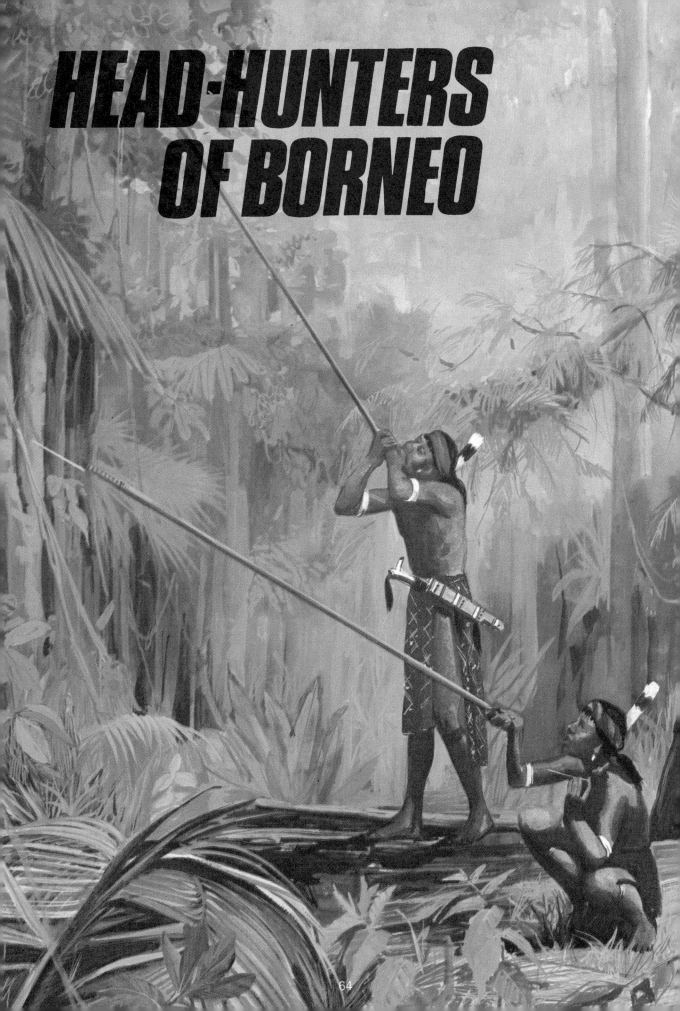

HEAD-HUNTERS OF BORNEO

TODAY, THE DAYAKS OF BORNEO LIVE IN PEACE WITH THEIR NEIGHBOURS, BUT THEY ONCE HAD A REPUTATION FOR CHOPPING OFF THE HEADS OF THEIR ENEMIES IN BATTLE AND TAKING THEM HOME AS WAR TROPHIES.

SILENTLY, dusky hands parted the leaves in the dense jungles of Borneo, and a cocoa-coloured face peered at a party of white men pausing to rest in the sweltering tropical heat.

The native beckoned to some companions to come forward from their hiding places. They joined him and saw the white men . . . strange people whom they had never seen before and who could, perhaps, bring danger.

Blowpipes were raised. The warriors took aim. Poisoned darts hissed through the air and found their deadly mark on the unsuspecting party of men from across the seas.

Perhaps the white men were traders or missionaries. Whatever they were, they had come in peace. But the fierce tribes of the interior of Borneo had survived only by defeating or subduing invaders from other races, and they feared the white man as they feared all other strangers.

It is no wonder that these fierce blowpipe hunters had kept the white man out of the interior of their country until the 1820s, when exploration of the river valleys began. For they were the aboriginal natives, the Dayaks, with a reputation for chopping off their enemies' heads in battle and taking them home as war trophies.

Dutch traders discovered this in 1669, when they were attacked and murdered. British merchants were wiped out in 1707, and Portuguese missionaries trying to penetrate into the interior to reach the Dayaks were also murdered.

Today, however, the Dayaks live in peace with their neighbours. Their blowpipes are used for hunting for food, and head-hunting has become merely a part of their colourful history.

Their large island of the East Indian Archipelago in the South China Sea, five times bigger than England and Wales together, is split into four states or protectorates. Dayaks, Malays and Chinese, with a sprinkling of other races, make up the population.

Of these people, the most appealing—because they retain a very strong link with the primitive past—are the Dayaks. These are split into two hundred tribes, all with different customs.

Their homes are communal houses called longhouses or *lamins*, built in a clearing in dense jungle. Rice is their staple diet, and the whole community sows the crop.

First the jungle is cleared and the ground cleaned, then the men walk in lines making holes for the seed with pointed sticks. Women and children follow them, throwing ten rice seeds into each hole from baskets or bamboo tubes. The jungle ground is too poor to produce more than one crop, so a new clearing must be made each year.

All this sounds a strangely peaceful way of life for people who were once relentless fighters. For, in the old days, to gain merit in the eyes of his womenfolk, a warrior would cut off the head of an enemy he had killed and hang it from the rafter of the longhouse as a trophy.

This horrible practice has died out, but the Dayaks still worship the spirits of their ancestors because they believe the dead possess mystical powers denied to the living.

Their hunting instincts remain, however, and their victims are wild boar and small tree-martens, which provide food. Their only weapon is a six foot blowpipe, through which they blow wooden darts coated with poisonous sap. At other times, the pipe can be used as a spear, with a sharp point bound to the muzzle.

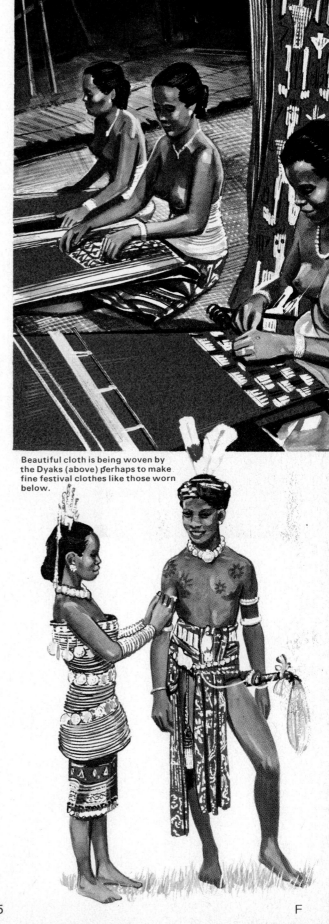

Beautiful cloth is being woven by the Dyaks (above) perhaps to make fine festival clothes like those worn below.

To keep themselves safe from wandering animals, and to raise themselves above the flood levels, the Dayaks' long-houses are raised on poles six feet high, with steps leading to a veranda. Animals—black and white pigs, dogs, cats and chickens—are kept in the space underneath. In these homes on stilts, each family has a separate room, but the veranda is used communally for work and play.

Great use is made of the bamboo plant, which grows freely in the Borneo jungles. Hats are woven from it, and musical instruments are made from the stem.

One explorer, Dr. Alfred Wallace, was amazed by the variety of uses to which bamboo is put. Not only are the houses made of bamboo, he says, but they are furnished throughout with articles made from it. Even the cooking vessels are made from it, and a single reed makes several cups and bowls.

Bamboo is a giant grass and some species reach a height of over a hundred feet, and have a stem more than three feet round. Girls carry water in bamboo tubes strapped to their backs in a woven bamboo basket.

Hollowed out bamboo tubes make fine musical instruments, and the Dayaks love music and play-acting. Often, they perform burlesques of their own tribal life or the manners of Europeans.

Dancing and music take place at night, when the veranda of the longhouse is lit by lamps which burn animal fat. Women dance to stringed instruments; then the men, arrayed in feathers, perform a bird dance which grows wilder as the audience yells encouragement.

Borneo has had a troubled history. Many people from many countries tried to establish settlements, or even to conquer the island. Hindus, Muslims, Portuguese, Dutch and the British tried to make use of the island, either for trade or war. The British took over the Dutch trading posts during the Napoleonic wars, returning them when peace came.

In the 19th century, Britain set up protectorates in the north of Borneo, and in the Second World War the whole island came under Japanese control.

After the war, northern Borneo became British, and the southern part joined the republic of Indonesia and was, in 1950, renamed Kalimantan.

Terrific upheavals for a primitive island . . . yet throughout it all the Dayaks retained their identity as a race of picturesque people, whose culture still retains a strong link with their mystical past.

THREE-WHEELING THROUGH AFRICA

"YOU'LL have to ride double-deck," said Mr. I. N. Patterson, a tall, pleasant American to the two friends he had just welcomed at the railway station in Abeokuta on the West Coast of Africa.

James Wilson and Francis Flood crammed themselves into the sidecar of Patterson's motor cycle combination.

"Great little machine," shouted Patterson, as the single cylinder motor chugged up a hill. "It's the only way to travel in Africa."

Wilson sat bolt upright and almost shot Flood out of the sidecar. Startled, Patterson stopped the machine.

"Motor cycles—motor cycles!" yelled Wilson, scrambling up and dancing up and down.

"What about 'em?" asked Flood calmly.

"Don't you see—only way to travel—motor bikes and sidecars. Three-wheeling through Africa, by the powers!"

Flood laughed. "Jimmie's having another fit. He thinks we're going to cross Africa by motor bike—that's all . . . Well, why not?"

And that was how it began—the Flood-Wilson Trans-Africa Motor Cycle Expedition, back in the 1930s, when parts of Africa were still the White Man's Grave, when the French Foreign Legion was still going strong in the Sahara, and the European nations controlled large parts of the Dark Continent.

Flood and Wilson were in Africa because they wanted

Undaunted by all the pessimists who said they would never come out of their adventure alive, and ignoring the advice of those who told them to swap their bikes for camels, Wilson and Flood set off on their great adventure.

67

adventure, and because Flood had an arrangement to write a series of travel articles for American newspapers. They wanted an experience that would be completely different from any other. Three-wheeling across Africa looked like being the answer. Nobody had ever done it before.

First, they had to find a couple of machines, and this they did with some difficulty in Lagos in Nigeria. Sturdy, little five horse-power, single-cylinder machines, with two-inch cooling fins and light-weight sidecars.

Like most of the people to whom they mentioned their plans, a motor-cycle dealer thought they were a pair of fools. "It's utterly impossible," he said. "No guides, no servant, no interpreters . . ."

But the dealer had a gleam in his eyes as he sold them their Triumph combinations. "Not much chance of coming out alive," he muttered under his breath—but if they did—*'Triumph Crosses Africa'.*"

He cabled Triumph in Britain, who said they could have the machines free. Dunlop gave them spare tyres. All the spare parts in Lagos were rounded up, even a spare cylinder and piston, extra chains, sprockets, roller bearings, axles. Two special luggage racks were made each to carry 16 gallons of petrol, a thousand miles' supply.

The machines had to be licensed. Maps obtained. Flood found what seemed to be an accurate Highway Map of Nigeria, only to be told by the Highway Supervisor that the only highways in Nigeria were on the maps. The others had all been washed into the Gulf of Guinea by the 70 inches of annual rainfall. They could get no detailed maps at all of Equatorial Africa, and their official permit to cross from Nigeria to Anglo-Egyptian Sudan seemed an anti-climax.

Undaunted by all the pessimists who said they would never come out of their adventure alive, and ignoring the advice of those who told them to swap their bikes for camels, they set off.

Ahead of them lay "impassable" creeper-entwined jungles, billowing hills of drifting sand, broiling, blazing heat and hundreds of miles of mud.

However, time enough to worry about the difficulties when they met them, they thought, as they kicked the starters and went pop-popping on their way.

Their route was to take them from Lagos in West Africa through Nigeria and what are now Chad and the Sudan to Massawa, the Red Sea port in Ethiopia. In those days, much of this was French Equatorial Africa or the Anglo-Egyptian Sudan.

They slashed at vines to clear a path in the jungles, gasped in steamy, airless forests and literally fought their way through impossible conditions.

One night they slept in the jungle, fearing attack any moment. They settled down between their motor bikes with a mosquito net slung between them. They had been told that the natives of Nigeria would slit their throats for a torch or a gun. But when they woke up next morning they found a bunch of bananas and a calabash of eggs beside

They had been warned that the natives of Nigeria would slit their throats for a torch or a gun. But when they woke up next morning, they found a bunch of bananas and a calabash of eggs beside them.

Soon, the whole village was dancing around the camp fire to the tune of Wilson's banjo. They had the best pow-pow in Africa that night.

them. Far from being murderous, the natives had been kind to travellers.

One of the things which kept Wilson going, although Flood was far from keen on it, was his banjo. Whenever he felt weary, he would take out his banjo, strum a few chords, and immediately feel chirpier.

One night he did this in the blackness of the jungle and heard an answering deep-throated *Bomm!*

"I almost went up through roof of the mosquito-net, I was so scared," he wrote in his book, "Three-Wheeling Through Africa".

Bomm! Bomm! The drums filled the air with jungle jazz. Taking up a torch and his banjo and slipping on shoes, Wilson went to join the fun and found thirty tribesmen dancing around a crackling fire.

African rhythms were booming out from a group of musicians playing tom-toms and horn and bamboo pipes.

"Hello," said Wilson, stepping out from among the trees. In five seconds everybody had gone. But when he twanged his banjo, the villagers returned and Wilson motioned them into a circle.

"Soon, the whole village was dancing around the camp fire to the tune of my banjo," wrote Wilson. "We had the best pow-wow in West Africa that night."

Flat tyres, broken springs . . . all sorts of things went wrong with their machines. But Wilson was an expert mechanic and was able to put them right. Once he constructed a forge to repair a sidecar spring. He lined an empty petrol can with clay to make a fire box and improvised a blow pipe from one of the machine's handlebars. With Flood puffing away as the bellows, he soon had a successful forge.

A moment of drama came when they had struggled through the searing heat of the Sahara, and almost collapsed pushing their bikes up mountainous sand dunes. They had less than half a pint of water and no idea how far away they were from their destination, a township named Lade.

They were weak, haggard, their faces lined and caked with dirt. The maddening thing about being lost and almost out of water, thought Wilson, would be to die, wondering if Lade was just over the next dune.

When night came, they rested quietly, saving what strength was left, and hoping. They had a sip of water, the first in sixteen hours, and a square of milk chocolate.

At four thirty in the morning, four donkeys came plodding over the hill followed by a weary driver. From him they learned that they were on the right trail for Lade after all. In fact, it was less than a mile away and, when they heard of their plight, villagers came out to Wilson and Flood with water jars on their heads. Soon, the two travellers had all the water they wanted—and more!

The rest of their story is equally exciting. When they arrived at Khartoum and, eventually, Massawah, Flood felt like a man who had awakened from a two thousand year sleep. They had been travelling in a world where age old customs still lingered.

But the twentieth century had been carrying on, as they found when they boarded a ship for India that served five meals a day and had a bath in every cabin.

You can read more about their adventures in "Three-Wheeling Through Africa" by James C. Wilson, published by Jarrolds in 1937. It is out of print, but there may be a copy in your local library.

TSUNAMI

THE WAVE OF DEATH

JAPANESE fishermen, hauling in their nets, were barely aware of a slight swell in the ocean. Busily, they emptied the generous catch into baskets and set sail for their villages.

Good prices would be paid for the fish. There would be food for all and a celebration in their homes that night.

But that slight disturbance of the sea had masked a deep, destructive force. Thoughts of joy turned to cries of horror when the men got home and found that their villages had been completely destroyed.

One lucky survivor told the fishermen what had happened. A monster wave had reared up like a watery mountain and engulfed entire villages. Homes were crushed. People were swept into the turmoil and drowned. Cattle perished.

Along other parts of the Japanese coast, the story was the same. The tremendous wave had killed more than 30,000. This was in 1896. But there have been other similar disasters which make people fear these dreaded destroyers.

The Japanese call them *Tsunami,* or "harbour waves". They begin with an earthquake beneath the ocean floor, like the monster born on 1st April, 1946, near the Aleutian Islands off the coast of Alaska. Shaking the ocean floor of the Pacific with titanic fury, it sent a million tons of rock down towards the centre of the earth.

A million tons of water surged into the cavern left behind and an immense crater 100 miles wide appeared on the ocean surface. Then the surface rose up again and down again, and soon a giant wave was rushing southwards at a speed of more than 500 miles an hour.

Terror struck Hawaii when the tidal wave reached it five hours later. Ships at anchor were torn from their moorings and swept on to the shore.

More than two hundred Hawaiians lost their lives, hundreds more were seriously injured and thousands were homeless. Yet, the strange thing was that ships sailing towards Hawaii on that fateful morning passed through the giant wave without being damaged. In fact, their captains and crews were hardly aware that anything was happening.

When the wave crashed into Hawaii, it appeared as a wall of water more than fifty feet high. But in the vast expanse of the ocean, this size was very small compared to the one hundred mile length of the wave, which then became little more than a gentle swell on an otherwise calm sea.

Since this disaster, the problems of Tsunami forecasting have been seriously considered by scientists, particularly by Japanese scientists who have very special reasons to fear these killers.

It was a lucky chance which finally led to a way of making accurate forecasts of Tsunami. A conference of scientists was taking place in Hawaii on the very day that the 1946 disaster occurred. The scientists actually saw the "April Fool" Tsunami, as it has been called. What disturbed the scientists most was the knowledge that the wave had been speeding towards Hawaii for hours, although no warning of its approach had been received.

To make such a warning possible, a number of problems had to be solved. For many years, scientists have been using sensitive instruments to detect earthquakes taking place in various parts

of the world. These instruments, called seismographs, are very sensitive. An instrument in France or Sweden can detect, and measure the strength of, an earthquake as far away as Japan or Chile.

One problem for the scientists was that although all Tsunami are triggered off by underwater or landbased earthquakes, not all earthquakes trigger off Tsunami. So, seismographs could not be relied upon to give people a warning of Tsunami, or seismic waves as scientists like to call them.

People could not be warned about a Tsunami every time there was an earthquake, because there would be so many false alarms that people might ignore them when the real thing happened, and they would be taken unawares.

Finally, the scientists found the answer. This was simply a more complicated version of the small float or bobber sometimes used by fishermen to tell whether or not a fish is nibbling at a baited hook.

Two floats are used by the Tsunami warning system. One of them is a buoy which floats on the sea surface. Inside it is a radio transmitter which sends warning signals to coastal towns and cities.

A second buoy floats below the surface and is so made that it will move up and down when a Tsunami wave passes through the water. But it will not move when ordinary, smaller waves move past it.

These buoys are anchored to a single cable which stretches from the surface to a heavy weight on the ocean bottom. Extremely modern systems are equipped with small nuclear powered generators which can supply the radio transmitter with electricity for many years.

Once a Tsunami signal has been radioed to a shore station, a special computer analyses the message and works out the strength and speed of the approaching wave. Immediately, a warning is sent to all the coastal towns endangered and preparations for the safety of the inhabitants can be made.

No warning system can stop a Tsunami or prevent the damage it causes, but at least people can be moved to safety.

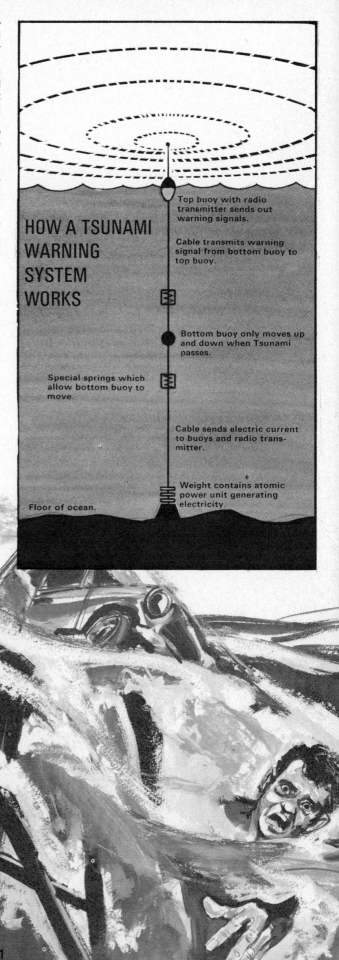

HOW A TSUNAMI WARNING SYSTEM WORKS

Top buoy with radio transmitter sends out warning signals.

Cable transmits warning signal from bottom buoy to top buoy.

Bottom buoy only moves up and down when Tsunami passes.

Special springs which allow bottom buoy to move.

Cable sends electric current to buoys and radio transmitter.

Weight contains atomic power unit generating electricity.

Floor of ocean.

OUR WORLD

If air pollution continues to grow increasingly worse, we may all have to wear a gas mask when we take a walk in the park.

The new science of ecology is a study of forests, oceans, the atmosphere, and other parts of the Earth's environment in relation to life inhabiting the Earth. Today, ecologists are discovering some surprising and disturbing things about man's own special relationship to the environment.

IN 1883 life flourished on the island of Krakatoa in the Pacific. Palm trees grew near the sandy beaches where shellfish made their homes. Exotic tropical plants flowered in the jungle where snakes and lizards lived silently in the undergrowth. Birds sang and a spider waited for a meal to be caught in its web.

Then, on a fine Spring morning a volcano, which had lain dormant for a million years under the island, suddenly erupted and blew Krakatoa to pieces. Dust rose into the air and formed a cloud which caused unusual sunsets all over the world, and the thunder from the explosion was heard a thousand miles away.

Life simply ceased to exist on the island.

Yet ocean currents still flowed towards the island, bringing seeds and floating eggs from other islands in the Pacific. More seeds were dropped by birds, some of whom were casual visitors, while others stayed as immigrants. Other immigrants, pythons and lizards, were strong swimmers and arrived by sea.

Today, Krakatoa teems with life, as it did more than fifty years ago.

For the modern ecologist the island of Krakatoa is an excellent example of a whole world in miniature. Because of the famous 1883 eruption many millions of years of history have taken place here in just over fifty years.

Yet the same kinds of things which have been happening here have been slowly happening in most parts of the

IN DANGER

Smoke from factory chimneys, combined with fumes from other manufacturing plants and exhaust gases from cars, is adding to the hazards of modern living.

world ever since life first began.

Rain poured down from the clouds and formed inland lakes. Rivers carried water down to the seas, gradually washing away the land, forming vast canyons, carrying soil to the river mouths to create deltas.

In some parts of the world earthquakes threw the land up into mountains, while in other parts the sea gradually rose, flooding the land and forming groups of islands.

As the land kept changing the living things also changed. Many creatures that lived in the sea gradually began to live ashore. Other creatures that lived on the ground started living in trees, some of these became able to fly through the air.

Many forms of life were able to change the land to a far greater extent than the weather and the oceans.

The tangled roots of mangrove plants growing in water collected sand and silt to form solid land. Small animals kept burrowing under solid land, destroying the roots of plants and creating deserts. And in desert areas hardy kinds of plants gradually formed acres of grassland.

Dotted over the Pacific Ocean are hundreds of islands which life has created. Thousands of generations of jelly fish have lived and died, and their hard skeletons have gradually formed reefs of coral, and these reefs themselves grew larger and became joined together to form islands. These islands then became new homes for animals and plants.

Some animals destroy the homes of other animals in their fight to survive. In some parts of Africa elephants, protected in forest regions, have been overbreeding, and have torn down acres of trees where thousands of birds built their nests.

A volcanic eruption destroyed much of Krakatoa island in 1883 (above) and life ceased until, with the passing of many years, plants and animals began to reappear. Will this pattern be repeated throughout the world in the future?

Industrial waste from factories, discharged into rivers, is killing the fish and may be a cause of other dangers.

HOW THE WORLD'S POPULATION HAS GROWN . . .

MILLIONS

BIRTH OF CHRIST	1650	1850	TODAY	2001 AD PROJECTED
250	500	1,000	3,700	7,000

Millions of cars are made every year. Getting rid of the old ones is a problem that leads to unsightly dumps or abandoned wrecks that despoil the countryside.

With a growing world population shown on the chart above, the problems of pollution and refuse disposal will be increasingly greater.

Pollution on the shores by oil discharged at sea is a danger to birds, fish and sea animals and causes considerable inconvenience to bathers. Clearing it (below) is a costly operation.

Still other animals have found homes simply by living on the bodies of larger animals. Tiny lice live in the feathers of some birds. The hermit crabs live in shells which have been discarded by other sea creatures.

For any living creature, whether it be a man or an insect, the environment is where "home" is. And home can be a house, a nest, a lake, or simply the whole world.

In fact the word "ecology" comes from two Greek words meaning *home* and *study*.

THE BALANCE OF NATURE

Animals feed on other animals to survive, but the animals they feed on must also eat smaller animals. Just what this means in terms of animal life is surprising when we consider what happens when human beings eat fish.

To put on one pound of weight a grown man must eat 10 pounds of fish. These fish must eat 100 pounds of tiny sea creatures to put on one pound in their weight. And the tiny sea creatures must eat 1,000 pounds of microscopic plants called *plankton* in turn.

Carnivores are animals that eat other animals, and ecologists have estimated that generally speaking carnivores slowly keep making the animal population of the world slightly smaller.

Vegetarians are animals (including some humans) who eat plants. Here we find a certain balance in nature.

Animals eat the plants, grow up and die, and their bodies decay and enrich the soil with compounds of nitrogen which can be food for new plants to grow.

The atmosphere, of course, is an important part of the world's environment, and it is here that for millions of years both plants and animals have cooperated in another balance of nature.

Plants absorb carbon dioxide when they grow and give off oxygen into the atmosphere. They also use a little oxygen, but only a very small proportion of what they produce. Most animals, however, use up this oxygen, but then they give off carbon dioxide to the atmosphere in return. So the atmosphere tends always to contain enough oxygen and carbon dioxide for both plants and animals to survive.

DOES MAN USE MORE THAN HIS SHARE?

Ecologists are now beginning to understand how both plants and animals have played a part in changing the environment and also using it to find food to eat and homes to live in.

Compared with human beings animals use a very small part of the environment for living in and building

homes. Birds use small amounts of grass, mud, straw, and sometimes a few twigs. Most land animals do not build homes at all, they simply burrow into the ground or live in caves, hollow trees, or shrubbery. Insects are active builders, but most of them use up very little material. And most fish are not builders, their home is simply the seawater surrounding them.

Way back in history when man lived in caves and used primitive tools to hunt and fish, he probably used and changed the environment to little greater extent than many animals.

Then man invented new tools and machines. He built houses and even huge palaces to live in, and began to quarry away huge chunks of the Earth's surface to get stone. He dug into the Earth for coal to heat his new homes and to work blast-furnaces to make steel for his new machines.

It has been calculated that in the last thirty years alone civilised man has used and changed more of the total environment of the world than he has in more than 5,000 years of his history.

Unfortunately man has taken much more from the world than he could ever put back.

Animals use water for drinking. But ecologists believe that in the 20th century man has used as much water in his factories and steel works, food-

The average family normally fills one dustbin a week with rubbish. In ten years, this total may have grown to five dustbin loads a week.

processing plants and railways and power stations than he has used to drink and keep himself clean for more than 3,000 years! And he certainly used much more oxygen to burn fuel in his jet planes and motor cars than he has breathed in since modern forms of transport were invented.

The petroleum, natural gas, and coal man has taken from the Earth can never be put back. By the year A.D. 2000 available supplies of these fuels could have been exhausted. It is frightening to realise that it has taken millions of years for these particular natural resources to be created by biological action, yet in less than three centuries man will have used them up.

Plants replace the oxygen in the atmosphere, yet man is busily reducing the amount of plant life in the world by cutting down forests. And chemicals from motor car exhausts are rising up to heights of 50,000 feet, forming a haze spreading over the whole world. Even now this haze is beginning to weaken the radiation from the Sun which plants need to manufacture oxygen using the green chemical chlorophyll in their leaves.

Many ecologists find it socially unacceptable that this waste of natural resources is directly the fault of only a small part of the world population. Today's estimates show that only about 10 percent of the world population is responsible for over 90 percent of this waste.

Even if we were not polluting the atmosphere and the oceans with chemicals from our factories we are in danger of running out of fuel. For although atomic power can replace coal, oil, and gas we are dependent on supplies of uranium, and at the rate we will probably have to use atomic power during the next century, it is unlikely that world supplies of uranium will last for more than fifty years at most.

It is curious that we seem willing to use vast resources of material and human ingenuity to make TV sets and motor cars, yet very little time and effort seems to be spent in speeding up new lines of research into ways of harnessing radiation from the Sun, a source of power which can last almost indefinitely.

Another fact revealed by many ecologists may have tragic results for mankind in the future: our production of cars, electric razors and tin-openers, washing machines and clothing is steadily on the increase, yet food production and the building of new homes just keeps pace with the rise in population.

Ecologists all agree that the world is in danger and the facts and figures are now available to prove it. Unfortunately scientists and governments and industrialists cannot agree on how the danger can be averted. But one thing seems certain: if our civilisation *is* to survive, then most of us will have to learn to do without many modern comforts. We may even have to stop riding in cars and watching TV programmes!

Nature took thousands of years to create the Grand Canyon of Colorado (above), but a green Welsh valley (below) was made into a wilderness by Man in a little over a century.

CAVES OF ADVENTURE

HAROUN Tazieff was helpless! Beneath him lay 240 feet of eerie gloom. More than 1,330 feet above him stretched the blackness of a narrow shaft which had been eroded out of the limestone rock of the Pyrenean mountains in France.

Ice-cold water splashed on to him from an underground waterfall as he hung suspended in the blackness on a strand of wire he could not see.

The winch hauling him to the surface after his adventurous explorations in the heart of a mountain had broken down. Frantic rescue teams on the surface were working to repair it. But meanwhile Tazieff hung helplessly in his harness, weighed down by a kitbag, helmet and tough, protective clothing, a microphone strapped to his throat to give him communication with the team on the surface.

Freezing air enveloped him as he hung limply in the black space, for he had switched off his lamp to save the batteries.

At first, he did not know what was wrong and he was furious. "How long have I got to hang here?" he shouted into his microphone. "Tell me frankly. I'm no coward."

The voice of the rescue worker on the surface was reassuring. "A quarter of an hour, perhaps," it said. "They're working on it now."

But the hours passed, and still Tazieff hung there . . . hours in which he had time to reflect on all the experiences that he and his companions had had in the Lepineux chasm, the deepest discovered in France at that time, in 1951.

Tazieff, a Frenchman, was a newcomer to speleology (the exploration of underground caves), although he was a distinguished vulcanologist, alpinist and geologist. He had joined this French expedition to extend his interests in studying the earth's resources.

In his book, "Caves of Adventure", Tazieff wrote, "The first perpendicular drop is truly formidable—more than 300 metres. It is tempting to penetrate thus into the heart of a mountain where the rumbling of powerful underground streams can be heard. But the lure of exploring the unknown is reinforced by practical interests, for it is a question of finding a flow of water, high above the level of the valley, that could be a source of generating power. The expedition of 1951 revealed the huge possibilities of a cavern and also the presence of an underground river."

Tazieff was in his predicament because of a bird. A crow had been seen emerging in full flight from a rock on a mountainside. Crows build their nests in places where there is a clear drop beneath them. This gave a party of exploring pot-holers their clue. Climbing down a cliff, they ran to the rock wall and discovered a pot hole. They widened it and dropped pebbles that vanished in the dizzy depths of an abyss. Thus was the chasm of Pierre Saint-Martin discovered.

It was down this perpendicular shaft that Tazieff was plunged into the depths of the earth. He was lowered on a cable and, once there, he waited for his companion, Marcel Loubens, an experienced underground explorer.

Loubens duly arrived, and the two men set up a camp in the rocky cavern. Next morning, they explored the passages and chambers. Their crowning achievement was to get to a depth of 505 metres (about 1,530 ft.), after crawling along

Tazieff hung limply in space enveloped by freezing air. Quickly he switched off his lamp to save the batteries.

The chasm of Pierre Saint Martin was discovered after a crow had been seen in full flight emerging from a rock on the mountainside.

terraces, climbing down their rope ladder beside rock walls dripping with moisture with Loubens calling enthusiastically, "This is fantastic," his words echoing from rock to rock.

The two men were safely brought back to the surface, and a year later they were again in the chasms of Pierre Saint-Martin. This time the underground party consisted of Loubens, Tazieff and two other men. Their job was to survey, metre by metre, a huge cavern they had found the previous year.

When Loubens' stint was finished, he put on his protective clothing and harness to be winched to the surface.

"Have a good trip," called Tazieff, as the cable stretched taut and Loubens began rising, his shadowy silhouette spinning on the end of the cable.

At ten metres, the cable stopped. The yellowish beam of Loubens' breast lamp flashed on and off.

A brief cry of distress, and in silence Tazieff watched the beam of the lamp dart down the shaft.

"A fraction of a second later, the sound of crashing filled my ears. Three steps away, Loubens' body rolled clattering past me," wrote Tazieff.

Something they had always refused to believe, always held to be impossible, had happened. The cable had parted. A fall of ten metres through space and another thirty rebounding from rock to rock brought Loubens' body to rest in an unconscious heap.

The cable was mended, a doctor was lowered, but Loubens was past help, and he was buried in a tomb of rocks amid the caves he had given his life to explore.

Andre Mairey, the doctor, and Tazieff could not let this sacrifice be in vain. Together, they decided to retrace Loubens' steps, for in much of his explorations he had been alone.

Together, they probed deeper and deeper into the mountain, along passages, through caverns, up sheer cliffs until they reached the base of the great limestone mass where it rested on the underlying carboniferous rock. This was the discovery Loubens had made. From this point onwards, there would be a succession of galleries leading to a gorge six kilometres away. It was a pot holer's dream. Loubens had proved that it was possible to enter the heart of the mountain at the top and come out again 1,200 metres lower, having gone through the whole mountain mass within.

But now the expedition was over. Mairey was waiting at the bottom of the perpendicular shaft and Tazieff was dangling in space, the tragedy of Loubens, in his mind, waiting to be hauled to the surface.

He hung there for four-and-a-half hours until the faulty winch was mended and he finally emerged on the mountainside. It was night, and powerful lights were shining. A camp fire was waiting to warm his chilled and cramped limbs.

Mairey came to the surface the next day after spending the night alone 350 metres underground, alone with the memory of Marcel Loubens!

The impossible had happened. The cable had parted and the sound made by Louben's falling body filled the air.

Our World Quiz

Now you have read the world section of this book, see how many of the questions you can answer in the quiz below. The answers are at the back of the book.

1 The continental shelf off the north-west coast of Norway has an evocative name. Can you say what this is?

2 How many ships from Fleetwood perished there in ten to twelve years?

3 Boats have been sucked to their destruction by whirlpools formed by clashing tides near the Lofoten Islands. What is this area called?

4 What is the name of the area on a trawler where the men de-gut and behead the fish?

5 Secret plants were grown on the Seychelles islands in the 18th century. Do you know what these were?

6 Who was the early explorer who laid claim for France to the 92 islands of the Seychelles?

7 Who declared that he had found the site of paradise in a valley on the island of Preslin, and what happened to him in 1885?

8 One of the islands has a landmark which is a replica of a famous British clock. What does this landmark represent and on which island is it?

9 Which Russian Tsar ordered the building of the Trans-Siberian Railway and when did work on this begin?

10 Tunnelling, hill cutting and bridges were avoided in the building of this railway and timber was substituted for steel wherever possible. Do you know why this was necessary?

11 The arrival of luxury trains turned the Trans-Siberian Railway into one of the world's mechanical wonders. What were these trains called?

12 Thousands of Australians trekked across the Blue Mountains to make their fortunes in the 1850s. What were they seeking?

13 What was the name of the pioneer whose discovery began this rush of fortune hunters?

14 The Kerr Hundredweight, the Holtermann and the Welcome Stranger all have one thing in common. Can you say what this is?

15 Between the towns of Kalgoorlie and Boulder in Western Australia is an area called "The Golden Mile" reef. Do you know why it has this name?

16 The Dayaks of Borneo once had a reputation for bringing home some unusual trophies from their battles. What were these trophies?

17 Great use is made by the Dayaks of a plant which grows freely in Borneo, and many things are made from it. What is its name?

18 What is the staple diet of the Dayaks?

19 Two explorers crossed Africa on motor cycles with side cars in the 1930s. What were the names of these men, and what did they call their expedition?

20 When they found thirty tribesmen dancing around a camp fire, one of them decided to join the fun by playing music to them. On what instrument did he play?

21 A monster wave reared up like a watery mountain and engulfed many Japanese coastal villages. What is this wave called?

22 Two buoys, one on the surface and the other below it, are used to detect destructive waves. How is their information transmitted?

23 The greater part of an island in the Pacific was destroyed by the biggest volcano in history in 1883. What is the name of this island?

24 The study of forests, oceans, the atmosphere and other parts of the Earth's environment in relation to life has a special name. Can you say what this is?

25 If a man eats ten pounds of fish, by how much will he increase his weight?

26 The world's resources of petroleum, natural gas and coal are expected to be exhausted by the year 2000 A.D. For how many years are the world's supplies of uranium likely to last?

27 What do we call animals which eat meat (*a*) or plants (*b*).

28 In 1951, Haroun Tazieff explored the deepest chasm discovered in France at that time. What is its name?

29 The exploration of underground shafts is a very dangerous undertaking. Can you name this hobby?

30 The chasm of Pierre Saint-Martin was discovered because near its opening was seen a bird which habitually nests high above a clear drop. What bird was this?

THE BARBARIANS

How savage, uncivilised and unwashed were the so-called Barbarians who demolished the ancient world of Rome?

Ferocious Mongolian horsemen erupted from the east at the end of the 4th century and cut a swathe of fire and blood across half the world. They were Mongolians led by Attila (left) who achieved many conquests over the Roman forces.

A HORDE of unwashed, shaggy bearded Germanic savages suddenly bursting over the Roman frontier to burn and loot and slay—this is the usual picture of how the barbarians destroyed the Roman Empire, but how true is it? How savage, uncivilized and unwashed were

these Germanic tribesmen, the so-called Barbarians who demolished the ancient world of Rome?

By the time the Roman Empire reached its greatest extent it included all the ancient centres of Mediterranean civilisation, Greece, Syria, Iraq and

Egypt, but it also covered much more. The Romans occupied almost all the Celtic areas of Europe, Gaul, which is now called France, Spain and most of Britain. Those regions not conquered by Rome were mostly inhabited by Germanic tribes—Scandinavia, Germany and Central Europe. There were, however, some Germanic tribes inside the Empire along the Imperial frontier of the rivers Rhine and Danube.

This was the situation to the north, but Rome also had enemies to the south and east. North-east were the Slav tribes, south were the Berbers of North Africa and the Sahara. Below Egypt were the ferocious Aetheopians. South-east were the desert warriors of Arabia while to the east the Persians had for centuries rivalled both Greece and Rome in power and civilisation. All were barbarians to the arrogant Romans who considered themselves the only truly civilised people on earth.

Every frontier was a source of trouble for Rome's hard-fighting legions, but it was from the north that the final disaster came. Here the Celts were more advanced than the Germans who were themselves more advanced than the Slavs. And

there was yet another group, a race of nomads who were not even heard of before they suddenly erupted from the east at the end of the 4th century. These were the Huns, ferocious Mongolian horsemen who cut a swathe of fire and blood across half the world.

Almost all of our information about these various barbarians comes from the Romans. But modern archaeology paints a slightly different picture from the one they give.

The Germanic tribes were farming folk who lived in villages and were ruled by kings whose government was often more democratic than that endured by the Romans under the bloodthirsty military dictatorships of the last centuries of Roman rule.

Those tribes nearest the Roman frontier were deeply influenced by Roman customs and art. They even had a few small towns that tried to imitate the styles of a Roman provincial city. Farther east in Denmark and eastern Germany other tribes like the Angles, Saxons and Lombards were only slightly influenced by Roman ways. Beyond them in southern Sweden and present day Poland were purely Ger-

The Roman leaders were proud of the prowess of their legions on the battlefield. But it took all their strength and courage—and the help of the German tribes—to stand up to the Hun forces.

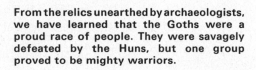

From the relics unearthed by archaeologists, we have learned that the Goths were a proud race of people. They were savagely defeated by the Huns, but one group proved to be mighty warriors.

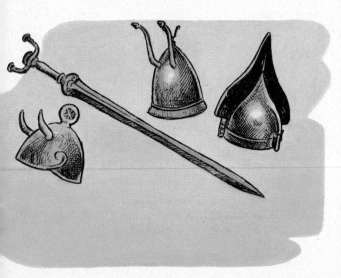

Rome's once proud legions were utterly defeated by the Gothic horsemen when the Goths moved menacingly south to create a turning point in the history of warfare.

manic peoples like the Goths and Vandals.

By the 4th century AD, the primitive little tribes who had been so resoundingly defeated when Rome first reached the Rhine and Danube, had gradually joined together through war or agreement into bigger tribes or nations. In fact, a new world was in the making beyond Rome's apparently eternal frontiers. Yet it wasn't these German nations that started the chaos which was in the end to destroy Rome—it was the Mongolian Huns.

The Hiung-hu, as the Chinese called their ferocious Hun neighbours, suddenly erupted in AD 363, no one quite knows why. They moved westwards, eventually driving the panic-stricken Germanic tribes before them to pile up against

the frontiers of Rome.

With war-crazed Hun horsearchers close behind, it's hardly surprising that the Germanic peoples didn't stop to ask permission of Rome's frontier guards before hurrying across the Imperial borders. It was like a game of skittles. The Huns, like a hard thrown ball, came crashing from the east to hit the first skittles, the Germanic tribes. These Germans then hurtled into the other skittles who were the Romans until everybody was flying in confusion all over the place.

It is hopeless to try to sort out all the chaotic tribal movements of the late 4th and early 5th centuries AD, so let's follow the fortunes of just one Germanic people—the Visigoths.

This western branch of the huge Gothic nation was living

quite happily in southern Russia near the shores of the Black Sea. They had migrated to this region over a century before from their original homeland in Sweden. For a while they ravaged the nearest Romans in the time-honoured Germanic way, then settled down in the 4th century AD. They picked up a certain amount of Roman culture and were converted to a strange, heretical form of Christianity called Arianism.

In the year AD 372 the Huns arrived. The Goths were savagely defeated. One group, the Ostrogoths or East Goths, stayed where they were and acknowledged Hunnish supremacy. Meanwhile the Visigoths or West Goths moved south across the Danube into Roman territory. The Romans, who were expending most of their energies in civil wars for the Imperial throne, agreed to let these Visigoths settle on condition that they defended the frontier against any further intruders.

Unfortunately the Romans

Making their way into Italy, the Visigoths sacked Rome in revenge for an Emperor's breach of faith. It was an age of chaos made worse by the warring nations.

also wanted these new inhabitants of their Empire to pay taxes. The Visigoths moved menacingly south. The Emperor of the eastern half of the Empire marched north from his capital of Constantinople, and at Erdine the two forces clashed on the 4th August AD 378. It was a turning point in the history of warfare. The Emperor was slain and Rome's once proud legions were utterly defeated by the mail-clad Gothic horsemen. The days of the foot-slogging Roman infantry were over, and the age of the proud medieval knight had dawned.

But that was far from the end of the story for the Visigoths. A year later they were defeated, but only when another Germanic tribe, the Franks, came to the aid of the Romans. Though beaten the Visigoths were still a menace inside the Empire. To keep them busy, various rival Roman Emperors employed the whole tribe as a mercenary army to fight Rome's endless civil wars. During this age of chaos the Visigoths gradually made their way through the Balkans and into Italy where they sacked Rome in revenge for an Emperor's breach of faith. From there they trekked west into France and finally into Spain.

JOINED FORCES

The Huns were still around under their most terrible leader, Attila, the "Scourge of God". In the face of such a foe even the rival German tribes and squabbling Romans joined forces. At Chalons in France in AD 451, a frightful battle was fought—neither side won, but the combined Germanic and Roman army did stand up to the Huns and survive. It was the first time this had ever been done. Attila swerved south to ravage easier regions, then retired eastwards to die of a burst blood-vessel.

As for the Visigoths, they settled down in Spain to develop a strange and brilliant civilisation of their own. It was partly German, partly Romano-Celtic and Iberian. Other Germanic nations settled down elsewhere—the Vandals in North Africa, the Ostrogoths in Italy, the Franks in Gaul, the Angles and Saxons in Britain. Some gave their names to new countries, the Franks to France, the Angles to England. Others faded into obscurity, but the Visigoths of Spain, though few in number, were to create one of the most brilliant cultures of Europe's so-called "Dark Age".

In the end the Visigoths were destroyed, but they had acted out one of the most heroic adventures in history, all the way from the shores of Sweden to the last battlefields of Spain, where the Muslim Arabs swept in and took what was left of Roman and Germanic culture to form the foundation of a still greater civilisation of their own.

PETTICOAT PIRATES

" AND what was your mother like, my dear?" "Oh, she was a pirate, sir!"

That would certainly sound a strange piece of conversation if you heard it today, but you might well have neard it had you lived in the 18th century when piracy on the high seas was common-place, because although most pirates were reckless, daring men, there were among them some equally fearless women.

One of these "petticoat pirates" was a girl called Anne Bonny who was born near Cork, Ireland, in the year 1700. Because her father wanted to keep her birth a secret, Anne was brought up as a boy.

Later, Anne accompanied her parents to Charleston in South Carolina, America, and when her

Anne Bonny went to sea with a band of smugglers and was soon mixing with notorious privateers and pirates. This was the start of her adventurous life as a pirate.

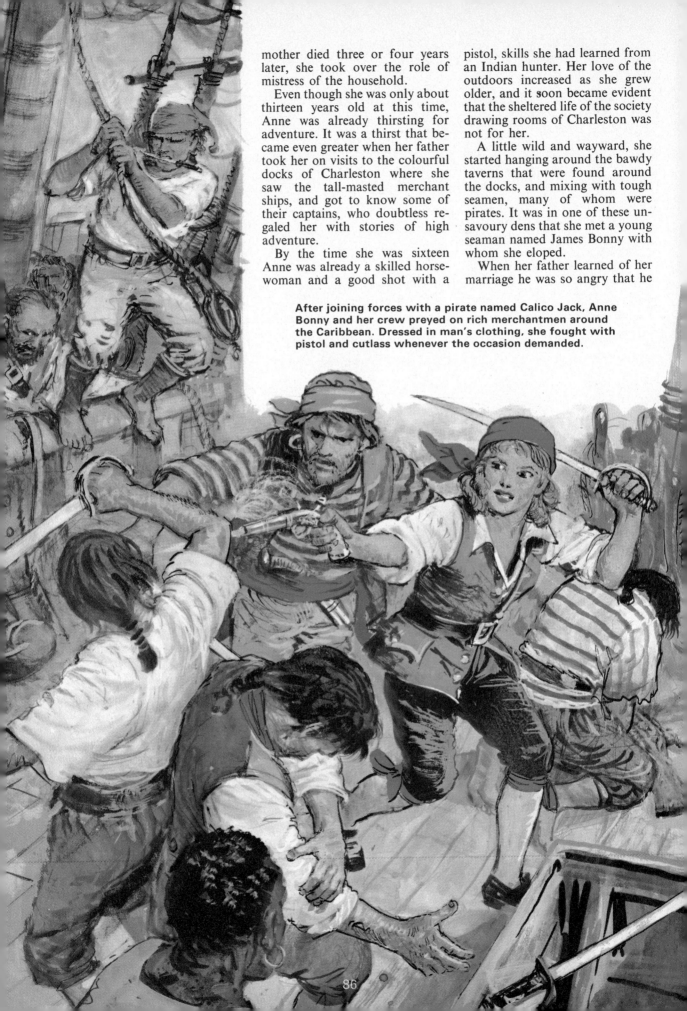

mother died three or four years later, she took over the role of mistress of the household.

Even though she was only about thirteen years old at this time, Anne was already thirsting for adventure. It was a thirst that became even greater when her father took her on visits to the colourful docks of Charleston where she saw the tall-masted merchant ships, and got to know some of their captains, who doubtless regaled her with stories of high adventure.

By the time she was sixteen Anne was already a skilled horse-woman and a good shot with a pistol, skills she had learned from an Indian hunter. Her love of the outdoors increased as she grew older, and it soon became evident that the sheltered life of the society drawing rooms of Charleston was not for her.

A little wild and wayward, she started hanging around the bawdy taverns that were found around the docks, and mixing with tough seamen, many of whom were pirates. It was in one of these un-savoury dens that she met a young seaman named James Bonny with whom she eloped.

When her father learned of her marriage he was so angry that he

After joining forces with a pirate named Calico Jack, Anne Bonny and her crew preyed on rich merchantmen around the Caribbean. Dressed in man's clothing, she fought with pistol and cutlass whenever the occasion demanded.

disinherited her, and Anne and her husband sailed off to New Providence with a band of smugglers. It was the start of her life as a pirate. Soon she was meeting and mixing with such notorious privateers and pirates as Calico Jack Rackham, Thomas Cocklyn and Edward Teach, who was known as Blackbeard.

READY TO FIGHT

Eventually, Anne left her husband and joined forces with Calico Jack. From then (it was about the year 1720) Anne and her new companion in crime sailed a sloop around the Caribbean preying on the rich merchantmen plying between Spain and the West Indies. Dressed in man's clothes she fought with pistol and cutlass whenever the occasion demanded.

By an odd quirk of fate, it was on one of these forays that another woman pirate, Mary Read, joined the crew. Like Anne, Mary Read was something of a tomboy as a child. Her brother died when he was only a baby, and Mary's mother brought her up as a boy.

Bored with the dull life she had at home, Mary ran away—and joined the Royal Navy using the name Mark. Later, she deserted and joined the army, still posing as a young man, until her deception was discovered and she was discharged.

The two women remained with Calico Jack's crew, fighting alongside them whenever a luckless merchantman was boarded.

TRAPPED

Their careers came to an end towards the latter half of the year 1720, when an armed sloop sent out by the Governor of Jamaica to capture Calico Jack, caught the pirates red-handed in a bay at the western tip of the island.

The story goes that the captain of the pirate vessel and the men in his crew put up little resistance, disappearing below when the fighting got too hot for them, and leaving the women alone on deck.

They were soon overpowered, and were taken in chains to Jamaica for trial. Both Anne Bonny and Mary Read escaped execution, but Calico Jack was hanged with a number of others convicted of piracy on the high seas.

Calico Jack was captured and sentenced to be hanged. As he was being led away, Anne is reputed to have shouted, "If you had fought like a man, you need not have been hanged like a dog."

As Jack was being led away, Anne is reputed to have shouted: "If you had fought like a man, you need not have been hanged like a dog!"

The petticoat pirates both went to jail for their crimes, and Mary Read died there of a fever. Anne Bonny was eventually released and returned to her home town of Charleston, where little more was heard of her.

THE GIRL WITH . . .
ADVENTURE IN HER BLOOD

When she saw the great airship flying in the light of the war-time searchlights, Amy Johnson knew that her future lay in the skies

THE little girl waited eagerly for the bus that was to take her on the first stage of her journey "to the North". She was a pretty child, with big blue eyes and curly brown ringlets; no fellow passenger could have guessed how she tingled with a longing for far-away places as she now checked the "provisions" bought after a raid on her money-box savings. The bag of toffees was still safe and sound.

Doubtless her wanderlust had

first been inspired by yarns her father had told her about his own adventures in the Klondyke gold rush of 1898. He had brought back barely enough gold to make a tie-pin for himself and a brooch for his wife; but his little daughter, Amy, never tired of hearing of his adventures in the frozen north.

The bus reached the end of the stage and the girl continued on foot. She plodded on until, completely worn out, she paused to rest by the kerb. Presently a car drew up and she heard herself being hailed by name. The driver was a friend of her father's. Would she like a lift home? Too tired to reveal that she was not supposed to be going home, she replied with a nod. Toffees and all, she was soon delivered at her door. But her adventurous spirit soon revived.

When she was eleven, the first World War broke out and it seemed a thrilling adventure to sit up long after bedtime, sipping hot cocoa in the cellar, "waiting for the Zeppelins."

One night she was missing. Anxiously her father rushed into the street and found his daughter eagerly scanning the skies for a glimpse of the great airship as it flew among the searchlights and the cross-fire from furiously pounding anti-aircraft guns.

Her father hurried her back to the cellar and safety, but the impression made upon the adventurous youngster remained for ever. The call of the North was forgotten—it was the skies for her!

The girl with the wanderlust, so fascinated by the skies was Amy Johnson, the first woman to make a solo flight to Australia.

UNKNOWN WOMAN

Shortly before breakfast on the morning of 5th May, 1930, Amy's small, green-and-silver Gypsy Moth biplane 'Jason' took off from Croydon Aerodrome. There were no big crowds to watch the event. Amy Johnson was unknown to the public, and only her father and a few members of the London Aeroplane Club were there to wish her well on a daring trans-world flight.

At a time when aviation was just struggling out of its infancy, to many people, the very idea of a woman flier seemed incredible. From the beginning of her career Amy had found obstacle after obstacle placed in her path.

When she was 16, Amy and her sister, Molly, went up on one of the 'five-bob joy-rides' which were the rage of the 1920s. The flight, however, was not the delight it promised to be.

"There was no sensation," recalled Amy. "Just a lot of noise and wind, the smell of burnt oil and escaping petrol . . . I was almost cured of flying for ever."

When she left school, Amy had to go to London to find work. She became a solicitor's typist at the grand salary of £3 a week—moved into a small flat and grew absorbed in the activity at a nearby aerodrome.

Eventually she presented herself at the London Aeroplane Club and asked to be given flying lessons. She was told that, with subscription and entrance fees, she would have to pay more than £8 before she could receive an hour's instruction. She saved as much as possible from her wages, raised money from her parents, and even borrowed a flying suit and leather helmet.

A year later, in September, 1928, she paid for the first of her weekly lessons. After 16 flying hours, she qualified as an amateur pilot with an 'A' certificate. She then trained to take her 'B' certificate, which meant she could carry passengers. She also became the first woman ever to sit for, and gain, a certificate as a Ground Engineer.

It was this background which led Amy to buy the £600 *Jason*. On the morning she left Croydon, the plane's open cockpit, which she labelled The Village Shop was crammed with everything she might need on a flight which could easily end with a crash into desert, swamp, jungle, mountain top, or even the shark-infested Timor Sea.

As she flew across Europe, and on to Baghdad and Karachi her attempt suddenly became world news. From the obscure office worker of a few days before, she leapt into front-page headlines from London to Sydney.

Amy's exploits did not disappoint the newspaper readers. They had all the thrills and excitement of a popular adventure novel. She crash-landed at Jahnsi, a station on the Indian plains, with her plane out of petrol. A wing was badly damaged, and the fabric need stitching. The repairs were performed by the village carpenter and the village tailor, whose nimble fingers worked with rare speed. No job, they told her proudly, was beyond their joint skills.

DAMAGED WINGS

After taking-off again, *Jason* flew into a blinding monsoon over the Burma coast. In her exposed cockpit Amy was battered and drenched to the skin. Still she battled on, and landed on a sports field near Rangoon. Again the plane's wings were damaged, and this time they were mended by students from an Engineering Institute, who knew little about aircraft but were eager to learn.

Finally, $19\frac{1}{2}$ days after leaving England, Amy arrived at Port Darwin, in Northern Australia. It was 24th May, Empire Day, and the whole world rejoiced at her triumph.

But Amy's story did not end in Australia. In 1931, she flew to Tokio, across Siberia, and back to Britain. The following year she beat by $10\frac{1}{2}$ hours the record set up by Jim Mollison, another British pilot, in flying to the Cape. She celebrated this success by marrying Mollison that same year, and together the 'Flying Mollisons' made a successful crossing of the Atlantic.

In the second world war Amy flew as a ferry pilot until lost over the Thames Estuary in January 1941.

Amy Johnson, the girl who had to fly.

UNKNOWN BUT WELL KNOWN

Who would mourn for the thousands of soldiers killed in battle who had no known grave? Worried by this thought, a Frenchman conceived an idea which has given glory to the world's anonymous heroes.

THE French army private walked slowly past the row of silent coffins. He paused near one; changed his mind and moved on. Then he stopped. The spray of red and white carnations he was carrying he dropped on the coffin in front of him. This was to be the one. The anonymous soldier interned within that tranquil casket had been elected to become the symbol of France's unknown dead — the representative of the many unidentified French soldiers killed in World War I.

A special train carried the body from the battle field at Verdun to Paris. On 11th November, 1920, all of France mourned as the unknown warrior was laid to rest. He was buried beneath the Arc de Triomphe in the Place d'Etoile—a place of particular honour. An eternal flame of remembrance was lit, and now burns continuously at the memorial.

The inspiration for this unique form of memorial came from Francois Simon, a printer from the town of Rennes in western France. In 1916 one of his sons had been killed in the fighting. Francois mourned deeply the loss of his son. But then his thoughts turned to those thousands

"BENEATH THIS STONE RESTS THE BODY OF A BRITISH WARRIOR UNKNOWN BY NAME OR RANK BROUGHT FROM FRANCE TO LIE AMONG THE MOST ILLUSTRIOUS OF THE LAND AND BURIED HERE ON ARMISTICE DAY 11 NOV. 1920, IN THE PRESENCE OF HIS MAJESTY KING GEORGE V HIS MINISTERS OF STATE THE CHIEFS OF HIS FORCES AND A VAST CONCOURSE OF THE NATION

THUS ARE COMMEMORATED THE MANY MULTITUDES WHO DURING THE GREAT WAR OF 1914-18 GAVE THE MOST THAT MAN CAN GIVE, LIFE ITSELF FOR GOD FOR KING AND COUNTRY FOR LOVED ONES HOME AND EMPIRE FOR THE SACRED CAUSE OF JUSTICE AND THE FREEDOM OF THE WORLD"

91

Italy's unknown soldier was buried in front of a massive monument to Victor Emmanuel II in Rome's Piazza Venezia (right). Soil from the battlefield of Ypres in Belgium forms the final resting place for Britain's unknown warrior in Westminster Abbey (below). An eternal flame of remembrance burns over the tomb of France's hero at the Arc de Triomphe in Paris (bottom right).

of soldiers killed in battle who had no known graves. Who would mourn for them? He conceived the idea of an 'unknown warrior' who would represent every soldier reported 'missing, believed dead', and every mother's son killed in battle.

Several other countries, in addition to France, adopted the idea. A Belgian unknown warrior was buried in Brussels between two massive stone lions on constant guard at the Colonne du Congrés. At the foot of the grave is a bronze bowl in which burns a perpetual flame. Italy's unknown soldier was buried in front of the massive monument to Victor Emmanuel II in Rome's Piazza Venezia.

Arlington National Cemetery, America's most important monument, set in 400 peaceful acres of rolling countryside beside the Potomac River in Virginia, was chosen as the resting place for America's unknown soldier. Selected from unidentified bodies taken from American cemeteries in France, the body lay in state in Washington before being buried on an anniversary of

Armistice Day (11th November), 1921.

The tomb bears the inscription, "Here Rests in Honored Glory an American Soldier Known But to God". A twenty-four hour guard is maintained at the memorial by the Honor Guard Company of the 1st Battle Group, 3rd "Old Guard" Infantry Regiment from Fort Meyer.

PROCESSION

In London, on 11th November, 1920, a funeral procession left Victoria railway station, and slowly made its way to Westminster Abbey. In the coffin of English oak lay the body of an unknown British soldier. It had been brought to England from Calais, wrapped in a battle-torn Union Jack, by H.M. Destroyer *Verdun*. The principal mourner was King George V, walking in the procession with the Prince of Wales (later King Edward VIII), the Duke of York, and the then prime minister,

Lloyd George. Queen Mary, Queen Alexandra, and the queens of Norway and Spain were also amongst the mourners. At Westminster Abbey the courtége was met by a guard of honour formed by one hundred holders of the Victoria Cross.

One hundred sacks of soil from the battlefield at Ypres were brought to England to form the warrior's final resting place near the west door of the abbey. The grave was left open for a week to allow thousands of mourning British people to pay their last respects. During this time many hundreds of floral tributes were presented to the nameless representative of the dead soldiers of Britain and the Commonwealth.

Each year on Remembrance Sunday the world remembers the more than a million dead of two world wars. The Unknown Soldier is a symbol of the nations' gratitude to the men who fought to save the world from oppression. The memorial is a concrete evocation of our hope that the same thing will never happen again.

TWO CENTURIES OF CYCLING

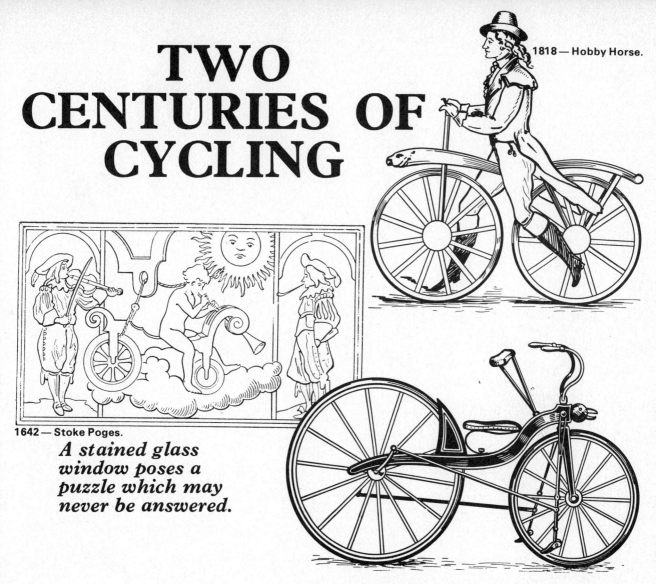

1818 — Hobby Horse.

1642 — Stoke Poges.

A stained glass window poses a puzzle which may never be answered.

1838 — Macmillan's bicycle, the first two wheeler with pedals.

1868 — Ernest Michaux with his "Velocipede".

THERE is a mystery in the church at Stoke Poges, Buckinghamshire. A stained-glass window, dated 1642, shows a boy riding what appears to be a bicycle more than one hundred years before the bicycle was invented! Is it the first bicycle? If so, who invented it? It has remained a puzzle for over three hundred years. Perhaps the truth will never be known.

What is known for certain is that in 1769 the people of London witnessed the first recorded use of a bicycle. It was called a "Phaeton". The rider sat astride the machine and propelled it by pushing his feet along the ground.

This form of propulsion was also used by the French Compte de Sivrac in 1791 when he produced his *Celerifere* (later re-named the *Velocifere*). Both wheels of the *velocifere* were in a fixed position so that steering had to be accomplished by leaning over at, what sometimes could be, a very dangerous angle!

The *velocifere* was improved upon by the eccentric German inventor Baron Karl Friedrich Christian von Drais de Sauerbronn in 1816. His machine, known as the *Drasienne* in France and the "Hobby-horse" in England, had a steerable front wheel. It became so popular in England that even the Prince Regent had one.

Twenty years passed before there was any further improvement in bicycle design. It came from a Scottish blacksmith, Kirkpatric Macmillan, who, in 1839, invented the first pedal-operated bicycle. The pedals, by means of connecting rods, drove the rear wheel of the machine. But the concept of rear wheel drive was ahead of its time and did not become popular.

93

Macmillan has, however, another claim to fame. In 1842 he rode the forty-two miles from Courthill to Glasgow in a two-day record-breaking journey. Near the finish of his journey he knocked down a child spectator. The Gorbals Police Court fined him five shillings, making him the first person in history to be fined for a cycling offence.

In 1865, Pierre Lallement, a mechanic at the Parisian firm of Michaux, designed the *Velocipede*. Pierre Michaux bought the patent and from 1863 to 1872, in the world's first bicycle factory, produced a large number of these machines. Charles Dickens, the author, had one. The English called them "Bone-shakers". This derogatory-sounding name is not surprising when one considers that the roads were extremely poor, and the bicycles had iron tyres!

★　　★　　★

The front wheel of a Michaux machine was slightly larger than the rear wheel. The front wheel of subsequent bicycles grew gradually larger and larger to enable the rider to travel faster with the same amount of effort. As a result the saddle had to be raised higher and higher until the rider was perched in a precarious position several feet above the ground.

These bicycles were nicknamed "Penny-farthings". Principal among them was James Starley's "Ariel" (1871) and John Beale's "Facile" (patented 1869 but not manufactured until 1878). They were certainly faster than earlier machines but also extremely dangerous and, with the increase in road traffic, something safer was needed.

The answer came with H. J. Lawson's "Bicyclette", first produced in 1879. "Safety bicycles" had been designed prior to this, but not made in sufficient numbers to gain public acceptance. The "English Mechanic" dated 30th July, 1869 contained an illustration of F. W. Shearing's safety bicycle, but it was neither patented nor produced. Many other weird and wonderful designs appeared but it was the

1871 — James Starley's "Ariel".

Whitworth Safety Bicycle, first produced in 1890, that proved to be the forerunner of the modern bicycle.

In 1897, John Boyd Dunlop, a veterinary surgeon, invented what was to revolutionise the cycle industry—the pneumatic tyre. His ten-year-old son had entered a tricycle race. To achieve a faster and smoother ride, Dunlop took some lengths of garden hose, formed them into rings and, having pumped air into them, fixed them to the wheels of the boy's tricycle.

Dunlop patented his idea in 1888 and found, much to his surprise, that in 1845 R. W. Thomson had invented a pneumatic tyre for use on coaches but the idea had not been developed. In 1888, the French brothers André and Édouard Michelin improved Dunlop's invention by producing a tyre that could be removed from the rim for repair.

The bicycle remained a popular form of transport until the 1950s when increased affluence brought the car within the reach of most people. Popularity continued to decline rapidly until 1962. Then Alex Moulton developed his small wheel bicycle with rubber suspension system. This revolutionary design was a sell-out that breathed new life into the cycle industry, and marked the comeback of the bicycle.

1878 — John Beale's "Facile"
(first patented in 1869).

Over eighty years separate the bicycle shown on the left, probably a Humber or Rudge-Whitworth Safety bicycle, from the streamlined racing machines of today.

THEY SAW IT HAPPEN

Their memories still alive with the sound of battle, the fiery ruins of a blazing London or the stench and terror of a deadly plague, only those who have lived through them can describe the great and stirring moments of history.

The Great Plague

By DANIEL DEFOE

London and other parts of England were swept by a terrible plague of bubonic fever in 1665. It killed 68,586 people, according to the official count, and probably more. At the time, James Foe was supplying sheep and cattle to the London food market, and the tales that he told to his son Daniel, who was then four, may have formed the basis for "A Journal of the Plague Year", a vivid contemporary description of the horror which hit the capital.

Passing through Token House Yard in Lothbury, all of a sudden a casement violently opened just over my head. A woman gave three frightful screeches and then cried, "Oh! Death, death, death!" in a most inimitable tone and which struck me with horror and a chillness in my very blood.

There was nobody to be seen in the whole street, neither did any other window open, for people had no curiosity now, in any case, nor could anybody help one another, so I went on to pass into Bell Alley.

Just in Bell Alley, on the right hand of the passage, there was a more terrible cry than that, though it was not so directed out of the window. But the whole family was in a terrible fright. I could hear women and children run screaming about the rooms like distracted, when a garret window opened.

Somebody from a window on the other side of the alley called and asked, "What is the matter?" Upon which, from the first window, it was answered, "Oh Lord, my old master has hanged himself."

The other asked again, "Is he quite dead?" and the first answered, "Ay, ay, quite dead; quite dead and cold."

But this is but one. It is scarcely credible what dreadful cases happened in particular families every day. People in the rage of the distemper or in the torment of their swellings, which was indeed intolerable, running out of their own government (out of their minds), raving and distracted, and oftentimes laying violent hands upon themselves, throwing themselves out of their windows, shooting themselves &c. Mothers murdering their own children in their lunacy, some dying of mere grief, as a passion, some of mere fright and surprise without any infection at all, others frightened into idiocy and foolish distractions, some into despair and lunacy, others into melancholy madness.

The pain of swelling was in particular very violent and to some intolerable. The physicians and surgeons may be said to have tortured many poor creatures, even to death.

We had at this time a great many frightful stories told us of nurses and watchmen who looked after the dying people, that is to say hired nurses who attended infected people, using them barbarously, starving them, smothering them or by other wicked means hastening their end, that is to say murdering them.

★ ★ ★

And watchmen being set to guard houses that were shut up, when there has been but one person left, and perhaps that one lying sick, that they have broken in and murdered that body, and immediately thrown them out into the dead cart, and so they have gone scarce cold to the grave.

The Great Fire of London

By SAMUEL PEPYS

2nd September (Lord's Day).
Jane (his maid) called us up about three in the morning to tell us of a great fire they saw in the City; but being unused to such fires as followed, I thought it far enough off; and so went to bed again, and to sleep.

About seven rose again . . . and walked to the Tower; and there I did see the houses at that end of the bridge all on fire, and an infinite great fire on this and the other side of the bridge.

The Lieutenant of the Tower . . . tells me that it began this morning in the King's baker's house in Pudding Lane and that it hath burned down St. Magnus' Church and most part of Fish Street already.

Everybody endeavouring to remove their goods and flinging (them) into the river, or bringing them into lighters that lay off; poor people staying in their houses till the very fire touched them, and then running into boats, or clambering from one pair of stairs by the waterside to another.

I to White Hall and there up to the King's closet . . . I was called for, and did tell the King . . . what I saw; and that

In September, 1666, a fire broke out in the city of London. Fanned by a strong wind, it spread rapidly and blazed for four days. In that time, it destroyed 87 churches, including St. Paul's cathedral, and engulfed 13,200 houses and 400 streets.

What was it like to live in London during this holocaust? One man who can tell us is Samuel Pepys, who described it in a famous diary he kept.

unless his Majesty did command houses to be pulled down, nothing could stop the fire. The King commanded me to go to the Lord Mayor from him.

4th September
The sky looks all on fire in the night . . . Now begins the practice of blowing up of houses in Tower Street . . . St. Paul's is burned, and all of Cheapside . . .

6th September
Strange it is to see Clothworkers' Hall on fire these three days and nights in one body of flame, it being the cellar full of oil.

7th September
Up by five o'clock; and find all well. Saw all the town burned, and a miserable sight of Paul's church burned, and Fleet Street.

8th September
People speaking their thoughts about the rebuilding of the City. I was kept awake in my bed by some noise I heard . . . some people stealing some neighbour's wine that lay in the streets. So to sleep; and all well at night.

97

The Battle of Trafalgar

By VICE-ADMIRAL COLLINGWOOD,
Commander in Chief of His Majesty's Ships and vessels off Cadiz

Not since the defeat of the Spanish Armada in 1588 had Britain won so famous a naval victory as the Battle of Trafalgar in 1805. It was by this important battle, fought off the coast of Spain, that Napoleon's power was broken on the sea. Britain's great naval hero, Horatio Nelson, lost his life in this battle when a musket ball struck him in his left breast. He was commander-in-chief of the British ships.

ON Monday the 21st October (1805) at daylight, when Cape Trafalgar bore east by south about seven leagues, the enemy was discovered about six or seven miles to the eastward, the wind about west and very light.

The Commander in Chief (Nelson) immediately made the signal for the fleet to bear up in two columns, as they are formed in order of sailing, a mode of attack his Lordship had previously directed to avoid the inconvenience and delay in forming a line of battle in the usual manner.

The enemy's line consisted of 33 ships (of which eighteen were French and fifteen Spanish), commanded in chief by Admiral Villeneuve. The Spaniards under the direction of Gravina wore with their heads to the northward, and formed their line of battle with great closeness and correctness. But as the mode of attack was unusual, so the structure of their line was new. It formed a crescent, convexing to leeward so that in leading down to their centre I had both their van and rear abaft the beam.

Before the fire opened, every alternate ship was about a cable's length to windward of her second ahead and astern, forming a kind of double line.

The Commander in Chief in the "Victory" led the weather column, and the "Royal Sovereign", which bore my flag, the lee.

The action began at twelve o'clock, by the leading ships of the columns breaking through the enemy's line, the Commander in Chief about the tenth ship from the van, the Second in Command about the twelfth from the rear, leaving the van of the enemy unoccupied.

The succeeding ships breaking through in all parts, astern of their leaders, and engaging the enemy at the muzzles of their guns, the conflict was severe.

About 3 p.m., many of the enemy's ships having struck their colours, the line gave way. Admiral Gravina (who was directing the Spanish ships), with ten ships joining their frigates to leeward, stood towards Cadiz.

The five headmost ships in their van tacked, and standing southward, to windward of the British line, were engaged, and the sternmost of them taken. The others went off, leaving to His Majesty's squadron nineteen ships of the line (of which two are first rates, the "Santissima Trinidad" and the "Santa Anna") with three Flag Officers, vis Admiral Villeneuve, the Commander in Chief, Don Ignatio Maria D'Aliva, Vice Admiral, and the Spanish Rear-Admiral, Don Baltazar Hidalgo Cisperos.

The "Achille" (a French 74), after having surrendered, by some mismanagement of the Frenchmen, took fire and blew up. Two hundred of her men were saved by tenders.

Such a battle could not be fought without a great loss of men. I have not only to lament, in common with the British Navy and the British nation, in the fall of the Commander in Chief (Nelson), the loss of a hero whose name will be immortal, and his memory ever dear to his country.

But my heart is rent with the most poignant grief for the death of a friend to whom, by many years intimacy, and a perfect knowledge of the virtues of his mind, which inspired ideas superior to the common race of men, I was bound by the strongest ties of affection. This is a grief to which even the glorious occasion in which he fell does not bring the consolation which, perhaps, it ought.

His Lordship received a musket ball in his left breast about the middle of the action, and sent an officer to me immediately with his last farewell, and soon after expired.

★ ★ ★

Admiral Collingwood's despatch ends on this sharp and unhappy note. But it should be added that fifteen enemy ships were taken or destroyed. Of eighteen that got away, two were wrecked and four later taken.

No British ships were lost and the casualties were only 449 killed and 1,242 wounded.

Trafalgar was tactically Nelson's masterpiece as it ended Napoleon's threat of invasion and was one of the world's greatest decisive naval actions.

The Battle of Waterloo

By THE DUKE OF WELLINGTON

In 1808, Britain began a military campaign against Napoleon in Spain and Portugal. The leader of this Peninsular War was Sir Arthur Wellesley, later the Duke of Wellington. He drove Napoleon's forces back across Portugal and Spain, and Napoleon was imprisoned on the island of Elba. But he escaped, gathered an army, and fought a last disastrous battle—the Battle of Waterloo—in which he was utterly defeated by Wellington and the Prussians, in 1815.

THE position which I took up in front of Waterloo crossed the high roads from Charleroy and Nivelle and had its right thrown back to a ravine near Merke Braine, which was occupied. Its left extended to a height above the hamlet Ter la Haye, which was likewise occupied.

In front of the right centre and near the Nivelle road we occupied the house and garden of Hougoumont which covered the return of that flank. In front of the left centre we occupied the farm of La Haye Sainte.

By our left we communicated with Marshal Prince Blucher (of the Prussians) at Wavre through Ohaim; and the Marshal had promised me that in case we should be attacked, he would support me with one or more corps, as might be necessary.

The enemy collected his army, with the exception of the third corps, which had been sent to observe Marshal Blucher, on a range of heights on our front.

At about ten o'clock on the morning of 18th June, he commenced a furious attack upon our post at Hougoumont. This was accompanied by a very heavy cannonade upon our whole line, which was destined to support the repeated attacks of cavalry and infantry occasionally mixed, but sometimes separate, which were made upon it.

The enemy repeatedly charged our infantry with his cavalry, but these attacks were uniformly unsuccessful, and they provided opportunities to our cavalry to charge, taking many prisoners and an eagle.

These attacks were repeated till about seven in the evening, when the enemy made a desperate effort with the cavalry and infantry, supported by the fire artillery to force our left centre near the farm of La Haye Sainte, which after a severe contest was defeated.

Having observed the troops retire from this attack in great confusion . . . I determined to attack the enemy. I immediately advanced the whole line of infantry supported by the cavalry and artillery.

The attack succeeded in every point. The enemy was forced from his position on the heights and fled in the utmost confusion, leaving behind him, as far as I could judge, one hundred and fifty pieces of cannon, which fell into our hands.

I continued the pursuit till long after dark and then discontinued it only on account of the fatigue of our troops, who had been engaged during twelve hours and because I found myself on the same road with Marshal Blucher, who assured me of his intention to follow the enemy throughout the night.

Such a desperate action could not be fought, and such advantages could not be gained, without great loss; and I am sorry to say that ours have been immense.

★　　★　　★

These losses were truly immense, as the Duke learned later when the figures were brought to him. Britain and her allies lost, in killed, wounded and missing 22,976 men and the French over 30,000 men . . . a total of nearly 53,000 men in a battle which raged from ten in the morning until five in the afternoon—7,500 an hour!

This battle crushed Napoleon's hope of regaining power in France and of building an empire. He was exiled to the island of St. Helena, where he died six years later.

The Charge of The Light Brigade

By WILLIAM HOWARD RUSSELL,
Correspondent of *The Times*

Six hundred British light cavalry troops rode through the plains of Balaclava on 25th October, 1854, to attack masses of Russian infantry supported by thirty large guns on heights above the plain. For the British it was a ride into a valley of death in which few survived one of the bloodiest and one-sided battles of the Crimean War of 1854 to 1856. A horrified spectator at the slaughter was William Howard Russell, the correspondent of The Times *newspaper, whose graphic pen paints a vivid picture of the battle. The narrative begins with an order from the Quartermaster-General, Brigadier Airey, for Captain Nolan of the 15th Hussars to take to Lord Lucan, who was commanding the light cavalry division, instructing his lordship to advance his cavalry nearer to the enemy.*

WHEN Lord Lucan received the order from Captain Nolan and had read it, he asked, we are told, "Where are we to advance to?" Captain Nolan pointed with his finger to the line of the Russians and said, "There are the enemy, and there are the guns, sir, before them; it is your duty to take them," or words to that effect, according to the statement made since his death.

Lord Lucan, with reluctance, gave the order to Lord Cardigan to advance upon the guns, conceiving that his orders compelled him to do so.

The noble Earl, though he did not shrink, also saw the fearful odds against him. Don Quixote in his tilt against the windmill was not near so rash and reckless as the gallant fellows who prepared without a thought to rush on almost certain death.

The whole brigade scarcely made one effective regiment, and yet it was more than we could spare. As they passed towards the front, the Russians opened on them from the guns in the redoubt on the right with volleys of musketry and rifles.

They swept proudly past, glittering in the morning sun in all the pride and splendour of war. We could scarcely believe the evidence of our senses. Surely that handful of men are not going to charge an army in position? Alas! It was but too true—their desperate valour knew no bounds, and far indeed was it removed from its so-called better part—discretion.

They advanced in two lines, quickening their pace as they closed towards the enemy. A more fearful spectacle was never witnessed than by those who, without power to aid, beheld their heroic countrymen rushing to the arms of death.

At the distance of 1,200 yards, the whole line of the enemy belched forth, from 30 iron mouths, a flood of smoke and flame, through which hissed the deadly balls. Their flight was marked by instant gaps in our ranks, by dead men and horses, by steeds flying wounded or riderless across the plain.

DEADLY GUNS

The first line is broken, it is joined by the second, they never halt or check their speed an instant; with diminished ranks, thinned by those deadly guns which the Russians had laid with the most deadly accuracy, with a halo of flashing steel above their heads, and with a cheer which was many a noble fellow's death-cry, they flew into the smoke of the batteries, but ere they were lost from view the plain was strewed with their bodies and with the carcases of horses.

They were exposed to an oblique fire from the batteries on the hills on both sides, as well as to a direct fire of musketry. Through the clouds of smoke, we could see their sabres flashing as they rode up to the guns and dashed between them, cutting down the gunners as they stood.

We saw them riding through the guns; to our delight we saw them returning, after breaking through a column of Russian infantry, and scattering them like chaff, when the flank fire of the battery on the hill swept them down, scattered and broken as they were. With courage too great almost for credence, they were breaking their way through the columns which enveloped them, when there took place an act of atrocity without parallel in the modern warfare of civilised nations.

The Russian gunners, when the storm of cavalry passed, returned to their guns. They saw their own cavalry mingled with the troopers who had just ridden over them and, to the eternal disgrace of the Russian name, the miscreants poured a murderous volley of grape and canister on the mass of struggling men and horses, mingling friend and foe in one common ruin.

At 11.35 not a British soldier, except the dead and dying, was left in front of these bloody Muscovite guns.

Abridged from "*The Times*", November 14 1854.

A PANORAMA OF POSTMEN

Mounted messengers once rode their horses at the speed of the wind to deliver the mail of their royal masters. Today's postman rides a bike, but he is a no less welcome and efficient member of a vital public service.

MILLIONS of letters are posted every day. It is the postman's job to ensure that they are delivered correctly. Whether your letter is addressed to Å in Norway, or to Taumatawhakatangi-hangakoauauotamateaturipukakapikimaungahoronu-kupokaiwhenuakitanatahu in New Zealand, you can be sure that it will reach its destination.

As long ago as 600 B.C. Cyrus the Great, founder of the Persian Empire, established a postal system across the lands he had conquered. The mounted messengers of Cyrus rode fast and furious, changing horses at stages along their route.

The most efficient postal system of ancient times was the "cursus publicus" organised by the first Roman emperor, Augustus Caesar. The excellent Roman roads enabled the couriers in their swift light-weight chariots to convey the official mail at break-neck speed. Although the public helped to pay for this service they themselves were not allowed to use it.

Horses and camels were used to carry the posts of the Arab Kingdom in about A.D. 700. A fast service was provided by horsemen. A slower post used camels and foot messengers.

The Incas of Peru, 700 years ago, used foot couriers called "chaquis" to run between Columbia and Santiago with important government mail. The runners, stationed in small huts about three miles apart, could cover 150 miles in one day.

THE KING'S MAIL

The European monks of the Middle Ages had their own postal system. Messengers moved from monastery to monastery carrying parchment scrolls giving the news. At each monastery the local abbot would often add his own snippets of information. As the journey progressed so the scroll grew longer and longer. One ten-inch wide scroll, written in A.D. 1122, reached the amazing length of 28 feet!

Several innovations in postal communications were developed by the Mamelukes. Formerly the mounted soldiery of Egypt, they became the most powerful people in the Middle East during the Middle Ages. Their couriers were identified by a yellow scarf on which they wore a silver badge bearing the Sultan's name and an affirmation of faith from the Koran.

Robert Carey, Queen Elizabeth's messenger, wore a

When the Persians wanted to spread the news of their conquests they used horsemen, while the Greeks (right) used hired horse-drawn carriages.

red uniform. When the queen died in 1603 he rode like the wind to Edinburgh to notify King James VI of Scotland. The 410 mile journey took him three days. The king, later James I of England, knighted Robert Carey in recognition of his service to the crown.

During the same year a two-tier postal system was introduced in Britain. The fast service, or "packet" post, was for the sole use of the sovereign. For this the postmaster at each stage was required to keep two horses always at the ready. Speed was of the utmost importance when handling the king's mail. The slower, "through" or "thorough", post was not so important and private letters could be sent by this method.

Thirty-two years later the nature of the packet post was changed. It was costing the crown over £3,000 a year to run. In order to recoup some of this money, Charles I permitted the public to use the fast post at a fixed charge.

Towards the end of the 17th century the stage coach appeared on English roads. But the postal authorities were slow to make use of them even

A Postboy of 1774. Vunerable to robbers and badly paid, these postboys travelled far and wide over the ill kept roads of the time.

The London Bellmen were used to attract customers and would then deliver letters to a central despatch office at a charge of ½d. each. Above: A London Postman of 1911.

though the post boy system was proving unreliable. Mail had a habit of disappearing en route as not all the mail carriers were completely honest. Those that were reliable ran the risk of being waylaid by highwaymen. Even the infamous Dick Turpin did not consider it beneath his dignity to rob the mail from time to time. And, on those occasions when the post did get through, it was often late.

As the result of persuasion by John Palmer, a merchant from Bath, the government in 1784 agreed to a trial mail coach run from London to Bath. It usually took a post boy three days to cover the 119 miles. Palmer's coach, at an average speed of seven miles an hour (good going in those days), completed the journey in 16 hours. Palmer had proved his point.

The sight of the mail coach with its guard resplendent in scarlet coat, blue waistcoat, and gold-banded hat soon became a regular and colourful feature of the English country scene.

POETIC ROBBER

In America the stage coaches of Wells Fargo rocked across the country carrying passengers and mail. The cash carried was a great attraction to the hold-up man. Wanted posters were hastily printed in an effort to apprehend the wrong doers. The man responsible for the greatest number of reward posters was mild-mannered Black Bart who robbed 28 stage coaches single handed. His trademark was a mocking verse left at the scene of each robbery.

On 3 April, 1860, the American Pony Express was started. An immortal and heroic service that fired the imagination of adventuresome spirits in all parts of the globe. Hostile Indians, robbers, and tough terrain were only a few of the perils faced by the Pony Express rider. Unfortunately the advent of the telegraph killed off the service, after only 18 months, on 26 October, 1861.

Back in England the introduction of the first postage stamp on 6 May, 1840, heralded many developments in British postal services. The stage coach was ousted by the railway. Postal rates in Britain were made uniform at the rate of one penny per half ounce.

The letter carrier who walked the streets of the major towns ringing a bell, and collecting letters was also to change. In 1853 collection boxes were introduced and the letter carrier, in 1861, changed his scarlet coat and gold-banded beaver hat for a blue peaked cap and blue uniform similar to that worn today.

But no matter how he is dressed; whatever his mode of transport; or whichever country he belongs to; the postman is now a familiar and welcome sight all over the world.

HISTORY QUIZ

Now you have read the History section of this book, see how many of the questions you can answer in the quiz below. The answers are at the back of the book.

1
What is the mysterious object shown in a stained glass window in a church at Stoke Poges, Buckinghamshire?

2
How did a rider propel himself when using an early machine called a "Phaeton"? What other device used this same method of propulsion?

3
What improvement did the German inventor, Baron Karl Friedrich Christian von Drais de Sauerbronn make to the velocifere in 1816?

4
A nickname was given to bicycles which had a very large front wheel and a small back one. Do you know what this was?

5
Until what date did the bicycle remain a popular form of transport and what took its place?

6
What name is given to the anonymous soldier chosen by his country to represent the unidentified soldiers killed in a war?

7
A French printer had the idea of erecting a tomb in memory of soldiers who died without known graves. What was his name, and when did he conceive this idea?

8
What countries, in addition to France, adopted his idea? In which of these countries is the soldier buried in soil specially brought from the battlefield of Ypres in Belgium? How many sacks were required?

9
Who was the founder of the Persian Empire who established a postal system across the lands he had conquered? What was the date of this?

10
A postal system was organised by the first Roman emperor. What was the emperor's name and what was his postal service called?

11
Between which two towns did the Incas of Peru use foot couriers to carry mail?

12
On what date was the American Pony Express started? What killed off this service, and when?

13
What race of fierce people suddenly erupted from the east at the end of the 4th century to menace the Roman empire?

14
What race of Goths moved into Roman territory and sacked Rome, and into which countries did they go after this?

15
In what year was the emperor of Rome slain in a battle between the invading Goths and the Romans?

16
Ann Bonny was brought up as a boy. What was her father's reason for this?

17
Ann wore men's clothes and became a pirate. What was the name of the pirate she joined in 1720?

18
Ann and two other pirates were caught red-handed by an armed sloop. Who sent the sloop to capture them?

19
Ann and another woman pirate went to jail. What happened to the man pirate?

20
What famous naval victory was won by Britain in 1805? What was Nelson's position in this battle?

21
The enemy consisted of French and Spanish ships. How many vessels did they have altogether?

22
What was the shape of the battle formation adopted by the Spanish ships?

23
Who was killed when a musket ball struck him in the left breast?

24
When was London swept by a plague of bubonic fever?

25
How old was Daniel Defoe at this time?

26
In what year did a great fire break out in London and destroy much of the city?

27
Can you name the famous cathedral which was among the buildings destroyed by this fire?

28
What famous diarist has left us a vivid description of this fire? What was his plan for stopping the fire spreading?

29
Who was Britain's leader in the Peninsular War against Spain and Portugal in 1808?

30
After being imprisoned on the island of Elba, Napoleon escaped, gathered an army and fought a last disastrous battle. What were the name of this battle and its date?

A COUNTRY
ON CANVAS

While Holland was being torn apart by turbulent wars, artists like Jan Vermeer and Pieter de Hooch were painting peaceful domestic scenes showing people going about their daily tasks and enjoying simple pleasures. The painting below, by de Hooch, is called *A Dutch House*.

For a hundred years Dutch artists produced some of the finest works of art the world has known, making the 17th century the Golden Age of Dutch Art.

These artists chose for their sub-

One of Rembrandt's greatest works was the *Night Watch* which he painted in 1642, the most tragic year of his life. Ironically, it was this painting that marked the end of Rembrandt's career as a fashionable painter.

jects themselves and their country so that all their art is intensely national, so very much a part of themselves. But it was not just national pride that inspired the Dutch painters of the 17th century to draw their homes and landscapes.

Holland was then a staunchly Protestant country and would have nothing to do with carving statues or decorating church walls as the Italians were so fond of doing. Instead of thinking about miracles and saints they turned to the countryside around them and the people who lived amongst them.

It is when we realise how much these pictures of homes and landscapes mattered to the people of Holland that we can understand how art in Holland became something which was lived with and loved at home.

Almost every artist who painted during the Golden Age of Dutch Art seems to have completely ignored the terrible wars and oppression of this turbulent time in Holland's history. When you look at their pictures it is hard to imagine that while they were painting their quiet domestic scenes Holland was torn by political and religious strife and was at war with Spain, and later with England and France.

And what of the artists themselves? Of the great men who lived and worked during this time—the men who made it a Golden Age of Art—Rembrandt, Hals, Vermeer, de Hooch and Ruysdael.

REMBRANDT-
The artist who captured the secret behind a smile

The year was 1642, and the brilliant Dutch artist Rembrandt Harmens Van Rijn had enjoyed the honour of being the favourite portrait painter of Amsterdam for eight years. Commissions from the wealthy middle class had been pouring in constantly and Rembrandt had painted some magnificent pictures. He was, in fact, at the height of his success. Then things seemed to go sadly wrong.

For 1642 was a time of tragedy for Rembrandt. Only thirty-six years old, he felt that everything was conspiring to make his life miserable.

And yet he had been a fairly happy man until then. Born the son of a well-to-do miller, Rembrandt had a happy and comfortable childhood and showed his enormous talent for art at an early age.

After a year at Leyden University where he was studying Latin he showed so plainly that art and not letters was his calling that his parents took him away from college and apprenticed him to a Leyden painter. After three years he went on to study at Amsterdam, but six months later he threw down his brush and went home, saying that he was going to work his own way.

For the rest of his life Rembrandt was to retain this faith in his own abilities and talents. His dogged determination to be himself and to express everything which he saw in his own way was to make him the greatest etcher and one of the greatest painters the world has known.

What he saw was the human soul hiding behind the human face. He was able to capture all the subtleties of expression that pass over a person's face because his eye was sensitive to the very faintest shadow of change in the deepest feelings of his subject.

A smile can conceal the most wretched, treacherous thoughts, and it was part of Rembrandt's genius to be

Rembrandt: A Self-Portrait, painted in his early middle age.

Jan Vermeer loved to paint pictures of people carrying out solitary tasks. These two paintings, *The Woman in Blue Reading a Letter*, and *The Milkmaid* show the wonderfully luminous effect which the artist was able to achieve in all his paintings.

able to draw the thought that was hidden as well as the smile. To do this he spent hours studying the human face. He used members of his family's household, poor people whom he saw in the streets of Amsterdam and Leyden, and even turned himself into his own model, sitting before the copperplate, needle in one hand and mirror in the other.

GLOWING DARKNESS

From this tireless industry and cease-less study came a supreme mastery of technique. Apart from his ability to render every conceivable expression of the face, and his technique, Rembrandt's outstanding genius was in luminosity, which has never been found either in etchings or paintings before or since. Anyone can make light light and dark dark, but Rembrandt made his darks glow with light and his lights hold a peculiar soft gloom.

His genius did not go unnoticed. By 1632 his fame was growing so fast that he moved to Amsterdam where he began to paint portraits for wealthy merchants, and produce etchings for his poorer patrons. Apart from those which have been lost and his earlier studies which he himself destroyed, Rembrandt painted 600 paintings and drew 300 etchings.

But his popularity soon began to wane. Commissions began to come his way less often. The men who had lavished money and gifts on their favourite portrait painter no longer wanted him, and then the tragedy

occurred. His beloved wife, Saskia, died in 1642 and Rembrandt was heart-broken. Business rapidly declined and by 1656 he was bankrupt.

Buried by a mass of troubles, his home life broken up completely, and posses-sing very little money, his last years were darkened by loneliness and sorrow. But Rembrandt continued to work as he had done all his life, con-stantly and consistently. Nothing could prevent him from perfecting his art, and he was to produce some of his most wonderful masterpieces in the sorrowful and lonely evening of his life.

THE LITTLE DUTCH MASTERS

Among the great artists of the Golden Age of Dutch Art, Rembrandt stands strangely apart. There followed no "School of Rembrandt" after the artist's death, and perhaps it was just as well for no artist could ever really imitate such a supreme genius.

But all the other artists of that time, though they were not of Rembrandt's genius, were great in their own special ways.

Jan Vermeer of Delft was the most calm and peaceful of all Dutch masters. Very little is known of his life, but it seems that he was a very slow worker for only about 40 pictures are generally accepted as his. After his death he was almost forgotten for 200 years.

Like Pieter de Hooch, another artist who lived in Delft, Vermeer loved to paint the domestic scene. Both artists painted pictures of ordinary people going about their daily tasks or enjoying simple pleasures. We feel that we are having glimpses of people's lives, being allowed to sit in their homes and watch what they are doing.

This peaceful intimacy in art seems only to have existed in Holland, yet it was at the time when these two artists lived that their country was going through one of the most violent and turbulent times in its history. When you look at their paintings it is hard to imagine that Holland was anything but the most peaceful place on earth at that time.

The town of Haarlem in Holland pro-duced two artists who painted very different subjects. Franz Hals was, like Rembrandt, a portrait painter. He had a similar ability for capturing human expressions. Always his subjects are smiling or laughing but, like Rembrandt, Hals was able to draw the thought behind the smile. Life, thought, and experience are shown behind the twinkling eyes and smiling lips of the people he painted.

Jacob Ruysdael was also of the Haarlem school, but instead of portraits, he painted landscapes and holds the honour of being the greatest landscape painter of Holland. His paintings of the light-drenched rivers and canals of the Dutch countryside have an effect of mirage and mist which give them an unearthly beauty.

THE MUSIC MAKERS

IF you were a member of any of the large symphony orchestras that play to audiences all over the world, your life would be far from idle.

Along with ninety-nine other musicians you may be required to attend a rehearsal at London's Royal Albert Hall one morning and then give a performance of a different work at the Royal Festival Hall that same evening. The following day you may be back at the Royal Albert Hall to perform the piece you had been practising the day before. Other rehearsals will also be taking place—perhaps for a forthcoming tour of Europe or for a gramophone recording. And all

There is much more to being a member of an orchestra than simply playing music at a concert. The orchestra's public performance of a composer's work is the result of a great deal of hard work and planning, all of which goes on behind the scenes, well away from the public eye.

part of a week's work!

All this requires a perfect, smooth-running organisation and for much of this planning you yourself would be responsible. Efficient arrangement of transport, maintenance of equipment and the provision of music are the three most important requirements for the efficient running of an orchestra.

What, then, goes on behind the scenes of an orchestra? First of all, the orchestra must keep a large library of standard musical works, and in addition to

this will have to hire works that are less often played. The orchestral librarian has to ensure that each player is given the correct music. When an orchestra plays under a permanent conductor the parts are usually marked by the players with the expression marks which their conductor expects them to play. In this way the conductor's own interpretation of a work is always prepared.

Players are responsible for their own instruments and for keeping them in perfect condition. Transport-

THE SYMPHONY ORCHESTRA

A: STRING SECTION
B: BRASS SECTION
C: WOODWIND SECTION
D: PERCUSSION SECTION

Violin

Viola

Cello

Harp

Double Bass

STRINGS

.ing 100 instruments from one place to another can create many problems. When an orchestra travels from one town to another, or to another country, arrangements have to be made for transporting the larger instruments such as bassoons, percussion instruments and harps. And it's vital that they arrive at their destination on time. If you have arrived in Germany in one plane and your harp is on a later flight, you obviously will have no instrument to play at the concert!

Apart from this more practical side of running an orchestra there is, of course, the music itself. In order to maintain a high standard of performance orchestras have to practise continually, even though each player may know the work very well and has played it hundreds of times.

The exact number of rehearsals required for a performance does, however, depend on how well the conductor knows the orchestra and how well the players know the works.

Under a permanent conductor and with a very familiar work a single rehearsal of three hours may be sufficient. The conductor will remind the players of the tempo and expression he wants and then run over difficult passages.

With difficult or unfamiliar works as many as seven or eight rehearsals may be needed. The conductor will take each section in turn, and then run through the whole piece with the entire orchestra until everything sounds just as he would like it to. Only when he is completely satisfied will the rehearsal stop. Then, and only then, is the orchestra ready to give a performance.

ARRANGEMENT OF THE ORCHESTRA

If you have ever been to a concert you may have noticed that the orchestra is always arranged in a certain way. The players are assembled in a large semi-circle on tiers with the conductor in the middle.

The whole of the string section is arranged nearest the conductor; to his left are the violins, in front of him the violas and to his right the cellos and basses.

The woodwind instruments are placed on the tier above the strings at the centre of the orchestra; the flutes, oboes and clarinets in front and the bassoons behind.

Behind the woodwind are the brass: trumpets, and trombones are usually to the right and the horns to the left.

Right at the back of the orchestra are the percussion instruments, and the harp or harps stand behind the strings.

There are very good reasons why the orchestra is arranged in this way. First of all, every player must be able to see the gestures and the expressions of the conductor, and secondly, it allows the different tones of the instruments to blend well so that the tone colours of the orchestra will have their full effect.

There are four main kinds of instruments used in the symphony orchestra, the stringed, the wind, the percussion and the keyboard instruments.

THE STRING FAMILY

The stringed instruments form about three-quarters of the entire orchestra and include about 40 violins,

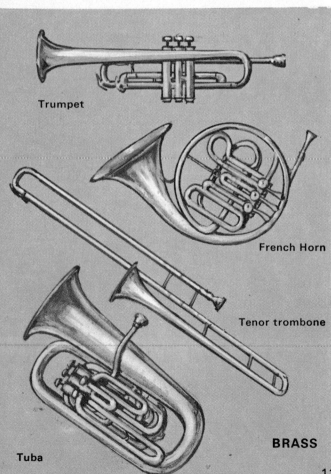

Trumpet

French Horn

Tenor trombone

Tuba

BRASS

Flute

Piccolo

Oboe

Cor Anglais

Clarinet

Bass Clarinet

Bassoon

WOODWIND

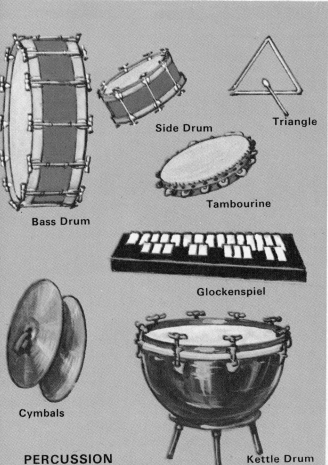

Side Drum

Triangle

Tambourine

Bass Drum

Glockenspiel

Cymbals

PERCUSSION

Kettle Drum

which are divided into first and second violins; 14 violas, 12 cellos and 8 double basses.

The violin is one of the most beautiful of musical instruments. The sound is made by drawing the taut horsehair of the bow across the metal or catgut strings. All the stringed instruments can be plucked instead of being made to vibrate by means of a bow, and this way of playing stringed instruments is called *pizzicato*.

THE WIND FAMILY

There are two types of wind instruments; the wood-wind and the brass. The woodwind instruments are the flute, the oboe and the bassoon and in all these instruments sounds are made by vibrating air within a tube. Cut into the sides of the tube is a series of holes which are opened or closed by levers and keys. This has the effect of shortening or lengthening the vibrating column of air inside the tube.

In descending order of pitch the trumpets, the horns, the trombones and the tuba make up the brass section of the orchestra. Like the woodwind instruments the sound is produced by air vibrating in parts of the tube, but the way in which the air is made to vibrate differs. With brass instruments the player presses his lips to the cup-shaped mouthpiece and depending how much the lips are tensed or slackened, a smaller or larger section of air within the tube is made to vibrate.

THE PERCUSSION FAMILY

Instruments where sound is produced by hitting or striking are called percussion instruments. In an orchestra these instruments are more noticeable because they are generally used for producing a loud, startling effect; at a climax, for example, when a clash of cymbals is followed by a roll of the timpani.

Instruments of the percussion section include the timpani, kettledrums, bass drum, side drum, cymbals, tambourines and castanets.

KEYBOARD FAMILY

The keyboard instruments—the xylophone, glockenspiel, celesta, vibraphone and piano are often classed as percussion instruments for they are also hit or struck.

The keyboard is the row of keys on a piano or organ which, when pressed down by the fingers connect with mechanisms which produce sound.

On the piano a hammer strikes the string, but on the organ air enters a pipe through a reed. This is why the piano is, strictly speaking, a percussion instrument, and the organ a wind instrument.

By striking several keys at once the player can make chords, which are different notes, produced simultaneously. The piano and the organ can each provide harmony which the other instruments do only when playing together.

The harp is a very beautiful instrument. Its tone blends with that of woodwind instruments and by means of pedals different notes can be obtained from each string. A brilliant effect is obtained when the player sweeps her hand over all the strings and this is called *glissando*.

TAKE A PIECE OF PAPER...

THE distinguished-looking knight seated on his horse on the left is a wonderful example of the skill of the paper sculptor.

With simple, cheap materials, he can create people of all shapes and sizes, from different periods in history, or from weird and magical places created out of his imagination.

Paper sculpture is not merely confined to the modelling of human and animal figures. There is hardly anything which cannot be made from paper modelling materials. Buildings, decorative designs, theatre sets, even a set of chessmen, can all be made by the deft fingers of the paper sculptor.

Everyone can try their hand at simple paper modelling, but the more advanced and intricate the work, the more patience and delicacy of touch you will need to make the model successful.

You can make almost every type of paper model with a few cheap materials which you can probably find in your own home: ordinary drawing paper, scissors, a "Stanley" knife (be careful—they are very sharp), staple gun (which you will probably have to buy if you need one), stapler pins, paper pins, drawing instruments, set square, compass, wooden ruler, metal ruler, and pencils.

On the following pages are some examples of the paper sculptor's craft, and a detailed step-by-step guide on how to make the knight and his horse pictured opposite. The instructions are drawn to

scale and your model can be as big —or as small—as you wish.

Do not get discouraged if your first attempt turns out less than perfect. Second and third attempts will be much more rewarding, and you may perhaps find that paper sculpture gives you everything you want in the way of a new, interesting, and artistic hobby.

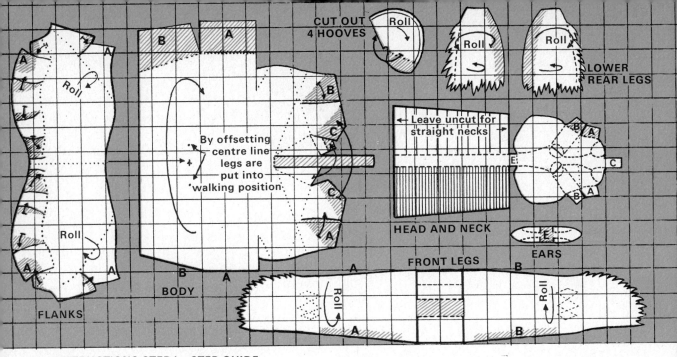

FLANKS · Roll · Roll

BODY — By offsetting centre line legs are put into walking position · B · A · A

CUT OUT 4 HOOVES · Roll · Roll · Roll · **LOWER REAR LEGS**

Leave uncut for straight necks · **HEAD AND NECK** · E · B A · C · B A

EARS · E

FRONT LEGS · Roll · Roll · A · B

INSTRUCTIONS STEP by STEP GUIDE

The weight of the paper is very important to make a model from the above diagram. The paper should be about the same weight as writing paper. Thicker papers would make folding and creasing very difficult in a model of this size.

The diagrams above are intended for scaling up to inch squares. Do this by covering a piece of paper at least 13 x 13 inches with 1 inch squares.

Cut all solid lines. Score all closely dashed lines. The open dots indicate the peak of curving surface. Use a quick-setting glue. Blue shaded areas are glued and placed behind position indicated.

GRAIN

Whenever possible roll or crease the paper along the grain. To find out where the grain runs take a small piece of paper and fold it across. Then unfold and fold it at right angles. The neatest fold will be that following the grain The other fold will buckle along the line of the fold.

Score the paper whenever a sharp corner or fold is required. Score from the reverse side of fold using a blunt knife or the back of scissors. Always use a ruler to keep a straight line.

When scoring curves gently follow line indicated as smoothly as possible.

To roll an extensive area of paper pull at a 45 degree angle from beneath the ruler held firmly down on a flat area.

Start by cutting out near flanks and rolling where indicated.

This helps form the shape required and holds the paper in place for gluing.

Cut out and form around a pencil the lower near legs. Insert into place as shown below.

2" · 5"

Cut tail from thinner paper. Cut the strands as finely as possible. Leave ½ inch of paper along the top to hold strands together. Apply glue along full length of ½ inch strip and roll tightly.
Stick to tail piece (A) and tuck in.

Angle cut of upper leg (B) to vary length position.

Roll the main body of the horse. Glue beneath stomach to join cylinder. When set, make up the chest of the horse. Glue tabs A and B on each side. Then tabs C glue face to face.

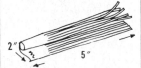

Cut out and roll front legs.

Glue piece between legs into position

beneath shoulder.

Make up four hooves

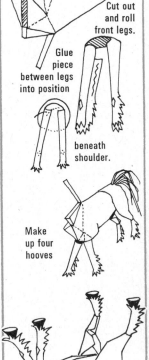

Glue and push into place. Then quickly stand upright on all fours and adjust legs so that at least three legs are on the same ground level.

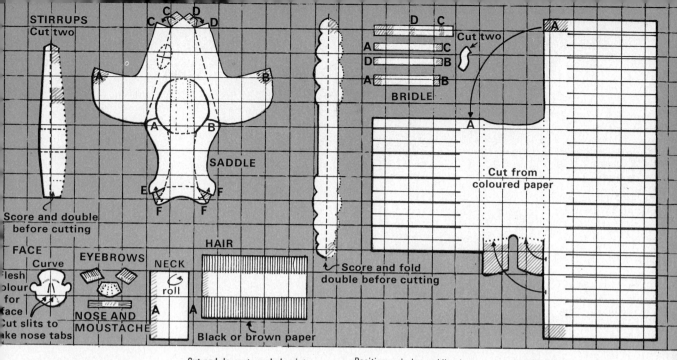

STIRRUPS
Cut two

C D
C D

SADDLE

A B

E F
F F

Score and double
before cutting

FACE
Curve

Flesh
colour
for
face
Cut slits to
make nose tabs

EYEBROWS

NECK
roll
A A

**NOSE AND
MOUSTACHE**

HAIR

Black or brown paper

D C
A C
D B
A B
BRIDLE
Cut two

A
Cut from
coloured paper

A

Score and fold
double before cutting

A

Cut out and crease head.

Push a
knitting needle
through eye-slit
forming upper
lid in and lower
lid out.

Glue tabs A. Then B tuck in
nostrils and pull flap C in line
with base of side nostril. Glue
flap C across
top of A flaps.

Fix ears
to
inside.

Glue flap from body down
centre of neck.

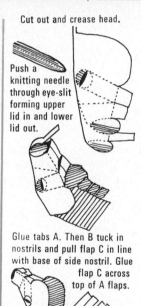

Your horse is now complete.

**Cut and decorate and glue into
position around horse.**

Cut out bridle and
reins.

Cut and score saddle. Glue A
to C and D to D. A to A next to
B to B. Complete by gluing E to
E and F to F.

Decorate as
you wish.

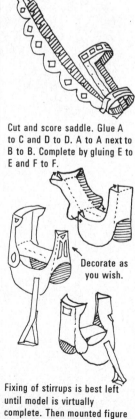

Fixing of stirrups is best left
until model is virtually
complete. Then mounted figure
can be positioned as required
Put feet into stirrups and glue
to saddle accordingly.

Position and glue saddle also.

The horse and its trappings
are now complete.

Cut out face and nose.

Give face a slight curl. Tuck
flaps of nose through slits in
face and glue from rear.
Curl and form neck around a
pencil. Cut out hair.

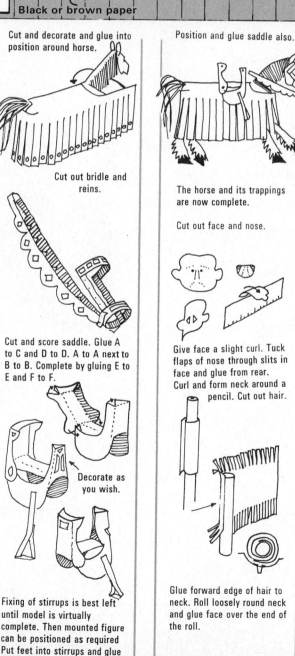

Glue forward edge of hair to
neck. Roll loosely round neck
and glue face over the end of
the roll.

Scrumple hair and whiskers.

Stick eyebrows and moustache
into place gluing solid areas.
Once set, twist them into
place.

Start helmet by making
into a cylinder, using
tube or roll of paper as
formed.

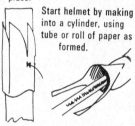

Use knitting needles or point
of a pencil inside visor.
Sandwich glue area between
needle and finger.

The plumes
should be
made of
paper which
has been
curled
and
twisted.

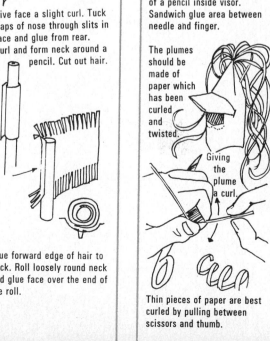

Giving
the
plume
a curl.

Thin pieces of paper are best
curled by pulling between
scissors and thumb.

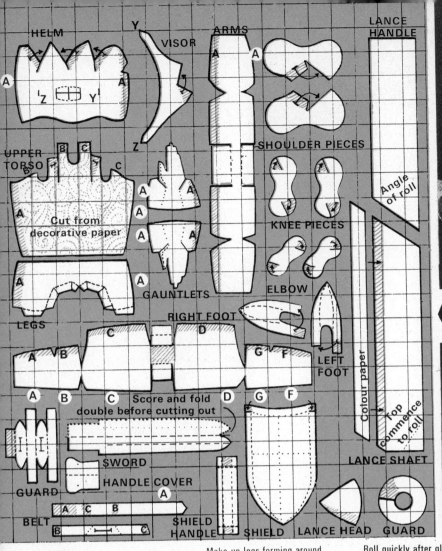

HELM

VISOR

Y

Z

ARMS

A A

A

LANCE HANDLE

Angle of roll

SHOULDER PIECES

Y

Z

Y'

A

UPPER TORSO

B C

C

A A

A A

A A

Cut from decorative paper

A A

A A

A A

KNEE PIECES

GAUNTLETS

ELBOW

A

LEGS

RIGHT FOOT

LEFT FOOT

A B

C D

G F

A B C D G F

Colour paper

Top commence to roll

Score and fold double before cutting out

SWORD

HANDLE COVER

A

GUARD

BELT

A C B

B C

SHIELD HANDLE

SHIELD

LANCE HEAD

GUARD

LANCE SHAFT

If possible cut all pieces on this panel from silver card (unless otherwise stated). Silver card is obtainable from most stationers.

Cut out and form arms around a pencil. Fold into bent arm position and glue.

Start upper torso by forming a cylinder.

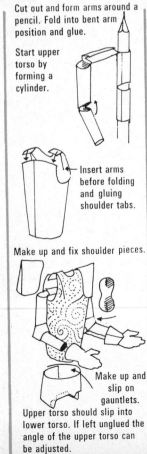

Insert arms before folding and gluing shoulder tabs.

Make up and fix shoulder pieces.

Make up and slip on gauntlets.

Upper torso should slip into lower torso. If left unglued the angle of the upper torso can be adjusted.

Make up legs forming around a pencil. Bend legs and glue.

Make up knee and fix.

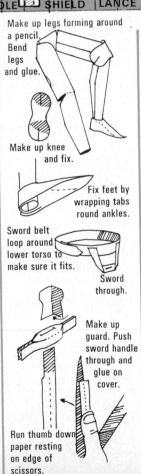

Fix feet by wrapping tabs round ankles.

Sword belt loop around lower torso to make sure it fits.

Sword through.

Make up guard. Push sword handle through and glue on cover.

Run thumb down paper resting on edge of scissors.

Roll quickly after gluing and fix in a colour strip. Otherwise the piece will be too stuck for the strip to fall into place.

Quickly form round a needle, remove needle and twist top as tight as possible, whilst allowing bottom end to spread.

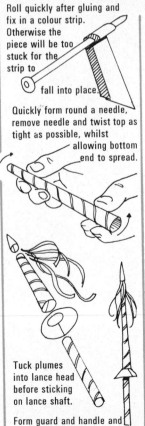

Tuck plumes into lance head before sticking on lance shaft.

Form guard and handle and glue all three together.

Make up shield. Add decorative motif.

Fold handle and glue rear of shield. Make up several pairs of hands. These are more easily glued to lance or sword. These can then be slipped over the arm.

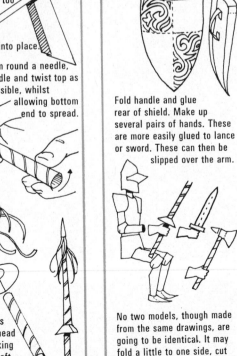

No two models, though made from the same drawings, are going to be identical. It may fold a little to one side, cut a fraction too deep. So always be prepared to cut or glue as you go.

JOSEPH CONRAD

The writer whose dreams came true

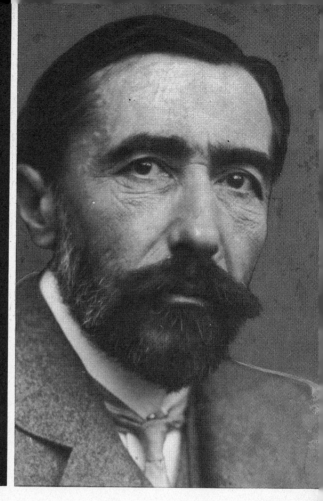

THE young orphan had been standing for some minutes before a map of the world which hung on the wall directly in front of him. The thoughtful expression on his earnest face and the excitement which showed in his bright shining eyes betrayed his inner thoughts. He was lost in a world of dreams and fantasies, of adventure and excitement.

Still dreaming, the young boy stretched out his arm and put his finger on a spot in the heart of Africa. "One day," he solemnly vowed, "I shall go there."

Konrad Korzeniowski had always longed to go to sea. As a young boy in Poland his imagination had been set on fire by wonderful adventure stories about the sea, and like most young boys, Konrad cherished a desire to travel the world. But with Konrad this "wanderlust" was something far greater and much more deeply felt than a passing boyhood fantasy. *This* little sea dreamer was deter-

mined that one day the dreams he weaved, would come true.

By the time he was seventeen, his dogged persistence in demanding that he be allowed to go to sea finally paid off. His uncle, who had accepted responsibility for the little Polish orphan, decided to consent to his ward's wishes and Konrad promptly went off to Marseilles as an ordinary seaman on a French ship.

NAME CHANGED

Four years later, in 1878, a cargo boat carrying linseed steamed slowly into Lowestoft Harbour in Suffolk. With only a few words of English at his command young Konrad went ashore saying goodbye to the crew of his ship who could not have known that the young Pole was later to change his name to Joseph Conrad and become one of England's greatest writers.

But many years of sea travel and countless adventures were to pass before Konrad began to

write his stories.

For some months he travelled between Lowestoft and Newcastle in a little 200-ton coaster which had the kind of magical name which exactly fitted into the young man's daydreams: *Skimmer of the Sea*. He soon qualified as an able seaman, and by 1880 had mastered the English language sufficiently to pass the first examination for officers in the merchant service. The new-fledged officer was then made third mate of a clipper which was sailing to Sydney in Australia.

Thus began the constant succession of adventures, roaming the oceans, which were to provide the writer Conrad with a rich storehouse of incidents to include in books which were to delight men, women and children all over the world.

With his passionate spirit of adventure, his craving for new horizons, and his love of danger, Konrad sailed the seas. To the magical Orient with its charms of a mysterious, legendary, far-

SOME OF CONRAD'S BOOKS

off land, across the Pacific and China Seas, and then to the place on the map which had conjured up so many of his boyhood passions—the Congo.

It was while travelling Africa that Konrad's health began to fail. He suffered four attacks of fever and although he continued to refuse to give up his travels, he was at last forced to return home. The immediate result of this voyage to the Congo was, as Konrad himself said: "A long, long illness, and a very dismal convalescence." For the rest of his life his health was to show the permanent effects of this African expedition.

NEW BEGINNING

The Congo episode and its deplorable consequences had far-reaching results and helped to turn Korzeniowski, the sea captain, into Conrad, the novelist.

It was while Konrad was convalescing that he picked up a notebook which contained a few hundred pages which made up the first seven chapters of his first novel *Almayer's Folly*. Written before he set sail for the Congo, these pages which had, presumably, been forgotten about, were now looked over again and Konrad decided to continue with it.

Unable to sail the seas which he loved so passionately and forced to rest, Konrad had time to think over the experiences of which his life was so full. Still only thirty-three, Konrad had a fund of physical and emotional experiences to draw upon— enough to fill the pages of many novels.

The sea dreamer had made his boyhood fantasy an adult reality and was soon to delight readers all over the world with his wonderful adventure stories.

LORD JIM

Conrad's most famous novel, "Lord Jim", is about a young English sailor who deserts his ship in a moment of crisis and is for ever after haunted by the knowledge that he can never become the kind of heroic figure he had once hoped he would be.

Miserably unhappy and forlorn, Lord Jim wanders aimlessly from port to port pursued by the story of his cowardice at sea. He finally reaches an island where Malay savages treat him as a demi-god.

But what little happiness he does find on the island is, sadly, short-lived. He allows the chief's son to be killed by a band of pirates and the natives can never forgive him for such a dishonourable deed.

So once again Lord Jim is stricken with guilt and shame. The realisation that he can never conquer his own cowardice prompts him to give himself up to the chief who kills him. That way he is at least able to die honourably.

This long, leisurely-told story has some magnificent descriptive passages in it and makes compelling reading because of the novelist's ruthless and merciless analysis of a man unable to escape from himself.

VICTORY

In this later novel Conrad deals with a man who is at odds with society. But unlike Lord Jim, the principal character, a Swede named Axel Heyst, has cast himself off from everyone by his own choice. He has deliberately divorced himself from a world in which he cannot exist.

With faith in nothing and nobody he wanders wearily around the globe in search for something to give purpose to his aimless existence.

It is only when he rescues a girl from the sea while he is living on a desert island that he feels the first glimmering of concern for a human being.

This encounter is followed by a succession of exciting incidents which, however, ultimately end in tragedy. Just as Lord Jim was able to find honour in his own death, so Axel allows himself to be put into a position that will destroy him. But he does this for a positive reason, for he has at long last found enough humanity within himself to lay down his life for someone else.

TYPHOON

During his exciting career at sea, Conrad had the misfortune to be shipwrecked and he chose this subject for the title story of a collection of tales called *Typhoon*.

This story contains one of the finest pieces of descriptive writing in the English language. In his detailing of the typhoon, Conrad brings his great mastery of style into play with such effect that the reader almost feels that he is part of the crew of the tortured ship, crashing through mountainous, enveloping waves that threaten to send it to the bottom of the sea.

The element of conflict, an essential ingredient of any story, is perhaps the most dramatic of all because it deals with man struggling against the harsh and hostile forces of nature.

AN OUTCAST OF THE ISLANDS

For the setting of this early novel Conrad drew upon his voyages round the Malay Archipelago. It was there that he met and heard about many of the strange characters which he was to portray in his stories.

While he was writing the novel in 1894, Conrad said that although he had no clearly-defined, well-thought-out plot, the characters and their moral plight were firmly established in his mind. "They are two human wrecks such as one finds in forsaken corners of the world."

The wrecks—the dissolute white man, Willems, and Babalarchi, the Malayan Muslim—are engaged in a struggle that must mean death for one of them.

Willems has offended the native code of honour, just as Lord Jim had offended the natives on the island where he lived, by his cowardly act. But instead of instant death which was Lord Jim's punishment, Willems' fate was to be stranded on a remote island from which there was no escape.

Masterpieces In Marble

To carve magnificent sculptures in marble. That was the dream of Michelangelo Buonarroti, an artist of such genius that he was to become the greatest sculptor the world has ever known.

The main figure of the tomb of St. Julius is this magnificent statue of Moses.

I N a corner of the Brancacci chapel in Florence, Italy, a young pupil of Lorenzo II Magnifico's School of Sculpture, sat deeply engrossed as he copied a work by the famous painter, Masaccio.

The young man, whose name was Michelangelo, looked up from his work to study the painting more closely and as he brought down his arm to carry on sketching, his friend Torrigiani, who was sitting very close to him, jogged his arm. Michelangelo moved his stool away and Torrigiani immediately took this as an insult. With a furious expression on his face, he stood up, yanked Michelangelo to his feet, and swung back his arm to bring the full strength of his massive fist crashing down on to the bridge of the young pupil's nose.

Stunned, Michelangelo swayed sideways, the Masaccio painting melting into a haze of crazy colours before his dazed eyes, as he felt bone and cartilage slide down his nose and then tasted blood and broken bits of bone in his mouth. Within seconds he had passed out.

When he awoke the next day, Michelangelo could still feel a piercing pain in the front of his face, and a throbbing ache at the back of his head. He crawled out of bed to look in the mirror. What he saw reflected was the most mortifying sight he had ever seen. Two huge, blue, swollen eyes in a crumpled face looked back at him. He had certainly never been beautiful to look at, but now, his face with its mass of twisted, disfigured features, was one of the most ugly things he had ever seen.

Michelangelo had always wanted only one thing: to carve magnificent sculptures in marble. Now that desire had become even more passionate as he contemplated his own ugliness, and he determined more than ever to produce beautiful works of art.

And what beautiful works of art they were! As a young pupil at the studio of the painter, Ghirlandaio, Michelangelo had always longed for the time when he would be able to use his hands to carve marble. He had no time for painting and although, in the Sistine Chapel, he was to paint one of the finest frescoes ever created, he always maintained that he was no painter.

But sculpture, marble sculpture, was his one consuming passion. It was to become his life. For weeks he would go with little food, and even less sleep, working at least 18 hours a day, and often the whole 24. For time did not exist for Michelangelo when he held a hammer and chisel, and could feel the power of the stone come to life beneath his hands.

After the violent incident with Torrigiani, Michelangelo began work on a crowded relief called "The Battle of the Centaurs", which showed a mass of twenty contorted figures wrestling with each other and which was to become a work that Michelangelo valued in his old age.

During his stay at Bologna, Michelangelo produced three memorable sculptures. Two statues of saints and one angel bearing a candlestick.

These early works of Michelangelo, though they show his exceptional talent, give only the slightest hint of what masterpieces were to follow. His first Pietà, commissioned by a devout nobleman for the French chapel at St. Peter's in Rome, made Michelangelo overnight the most celebrated sculptor of Christendom. And with very good reason. The master had chosen a theme which was very dear to his own heart. His own mother had died when he was

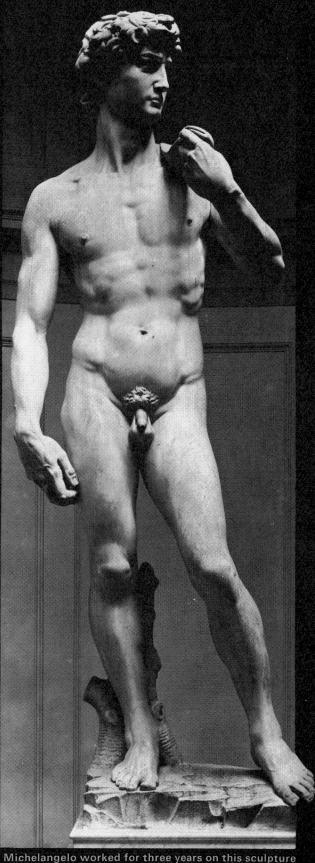

Michelangelo worked for three years on this sculpture of David which is considered his masterpiece. When it was unveiled in Florence the effect it had on those who had come to watch was that of a thunderbolt.

very young and he always imagined that she had been as beautiful as the Madonna. He raised the theme of the Pietà, the portrayal of Christ in the lap of the Virgin after his crucifixion, which had been used by countless artists before, to a height of spiritual and artistic perfection which has never been surpassed. Such harmony and skill in representing a divine presence had very rarely, if ever, been attained, and yet at the age of twenty-six Michelangelo was able to achieve just that.

For the next three years Michelangelo worked on the sculpture that has been considered his masterpiece. When the giant statue of the David was unveiled in front of the Palazzo Vecchio in Florence, the effect it had on those who had come to watch was that of a thunderbolt. There stood before them a powerful and almost fearful image of human life in all its majestic and breathtaking grace.

Michelangelo's perfect knowledge of the anatomy of the human body was unsurpassed in his day. As a young man he had crept into mortuaries in the dead of night to dissect the corpses which awaited burial. By doing this he learned how every organ of the human body functioned, and this is one of the reasons why his sculptures always seem to live and breathe as real human beings.

One year after the David had been unveiled, Michelangelo began work on the tomb of Pope Julius II. The main figure of this magnificent mausoleum is the eight-foot statue of Moses seated on a throne and lightly-clad in loose, flowing draperies. One arm upholds the tablets of the law, and the hand plays with the long cascading beard which frames a face charged with super-human energy.

Michelangelo was to build two other tombs before he died. These were the funeral monuments for Lorenzo and Guiliano de' Medici in the chapel which the sculptor himself built. When the chapel was completed after fourteen years of painstaking, interrupted work, Michelangelo was sixty years old. He was to live for a further thirty years but during that time he carved only a few more sculptures. The last years of his life were devoted to painting the Last Judgement in the Sistine Chapel, and to the architectural design of St. Peter's in Rome.

But he had already proved to the world that he was the greatest sculptor who ever lived, and since his death in 1564, there has been no artist of sculpture to compare with Michelangelo Buonarroti, and it is very doubtful that anyone ever will.

This beautiful statue of the Pietà made Michelangelo overnight the most celebrated sculptor in Christendom, and it is easy to see why.

122

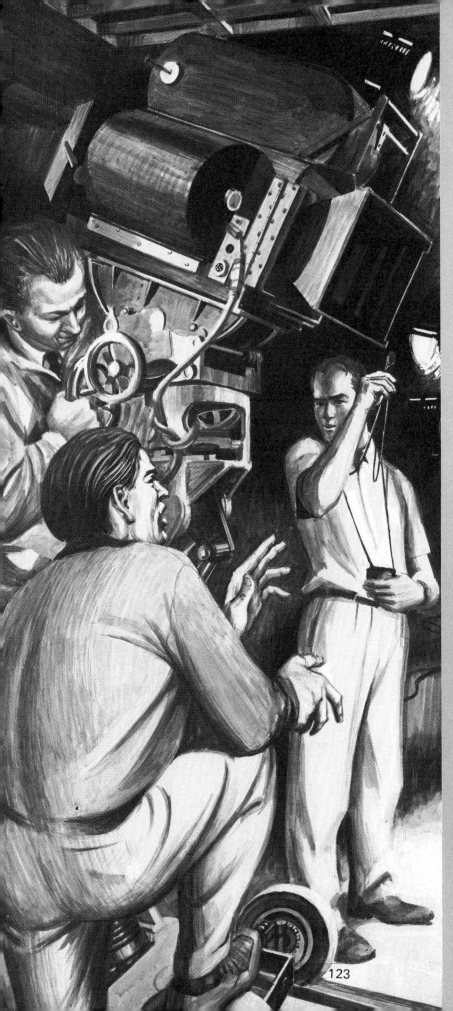

THE MOVIE MAKERS

IN a brightly-lit cinema of London's West End a rather impatient audience sits before the huge screen that is now hidden by a brilliant crimson curtain. There is a general murmur of conversation. An occasional laugh and frequent coughs rise above the voices and an air of expectancy permeates the whole room. In the minds of all is the question, 'When will the film begin?'

The lights begin to dim slowly, the curtain starts to move back and there is a short burst of shuffling as people settle down into their seats ready to sit back and enjoy themselves.

Then a hushed silence falls as the first chord of music blasts from the stereo speakers and an image slowly appears on the screen. The big film has begun.

Ninety minutes later, when the film is over, people start to get to their feet and edge towards the exits. Some of them are stunned into a thoughtful silence, others are talking nervously to their friends, and many are chuckling quietly to themselves at some amusing incident in the film.

Everyone has different thoughts in their minds as they leave the cinema. Some may be recapturing in their minds a highly dramatic part of the film, others may be remembering a scene which they found very funny, while a few may be thinking of no

The first cine camera was a small box on a tripod. Today it is a complex masterpiece of science and engineering like the one on the left. The film is in the magazine on the top; the lens is hooded to keep out the glare of unwanted light. In front of the camera an assistant is reading the strength of the light from a metre so that correct exposure can be given. Both he and the cameraman are receiving last-minute instructions from the director.

scene in particular, but of the film in general. All of them, whatever their thoughts may be, have been affected in some way or another by what they have just experienced.

Films are very complicated affairs, taking anything from five months to five years to make. During that time, thousands of people will have been involved in making a product that is designed to entertain the public for just ninety or so minutes. Good feature films are a peculiar combination of artistic talent, craftsmanship, engineering, technical expertise and hard cash.

No two films are made in exactly the same way, particularly if they are made by a different production team, or have different story-lines. But basically, the craft of film-making requires certain elements which should never be ignored.

Team work, for example, is one of the most obvious points about making a film. A painting may be the work of one artist, a book may be the

Part of the complex planning and preparation for a film involves set design. Here you can see the set designers and builders at work following closely every minute detail of the scene as shown in the original design. Below: the great moment for a 'take' has arrived.

A difficult location sequence is shot with a camera mounted on to a crane which can be raised, lowered and swung round with perfect control. This enables the swift-flowing action to be captured.

work of one writer, but a film is always the work of a great number of people. As with every team, there is a captain or leader who is responsible for the end product, but without his team there could be no product.

This leader is usually the producer, whose job is to obtain financial backing for a proposed film, to be in charge of the organisation and smooth running administration of it, and to be ultimately responsible for its success or failure.

The story of how a film is made begins with an idea for a subject. This could be a story that has already been worked out by an author or playwright, as in the case of a novel or a play, or it could be a story that has been specially written for the screen.

If the idea is taken from a published book or play the producer has to obtain filming rights from the publishing company before he can make a start on the film.

Then comes the very important moment when a director is chosen. Very often, a producer has certain favourite directors whose work he admires, or he may choose a director who has an obvious and definite talent for directing the type of film chosen.

Nowadays, directors are beginning to produce their own films and combine the job of producer and director, but generally, the two jobs are done by two different people.

Many people believe that the most important member of a film team is the director. And this is certainly justified. It is true that without his team, the director could not make his film, but at the same time, the finished film will owe more to him—to his talent, skill, judgement, and ability to bring the best out of

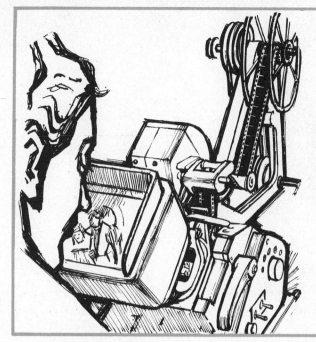

The vitally important task of editing the film. This is a moviola which is used for projecting both sound and pictures.

actors, than to anyone else.

The producer and director have to choose a script writer for the film. His job is to rewrite the story whether it is a novel, play or original screen story to make it completely suitable for a film. Sometimes, this may be a very difficult job, requiring a high standard of writing and a very specialised skill in editing a written piece of work.

If the script writer has to work from a long novel which has complicated plots and many characters, for example, he has to cut out many passages of the book, and often, many characters. This he has to do without changing the whole theme of the story, or losing any of its interest. He has to make sure that the story will stand up to these changes and

retain its continuity.

Once the basic story has been rewritten the 'Shooting script' has to be written. Everyone concerned with making the film has one of these scripts. It contains every word the actors will say, and also has every detail of every scene including instructions for cameramen. These instructions state what angles will be needed for certain shots. Such things as 'long shot' which is a scene photographed from a distance, or 'close-up' which instructs the camera to move closer, or 'tracking' which means pulling the camera back to give a wider shot.

While the shooting script is being written the chief cameraman is chosen. Again, the director may choose a man with whom he has

The 'dubbing theatre' where the music for the film is added or dubbed on to the soundtrack. The film is projected on to a large screen in front of the composer so that he can time the music perfectly with the action.

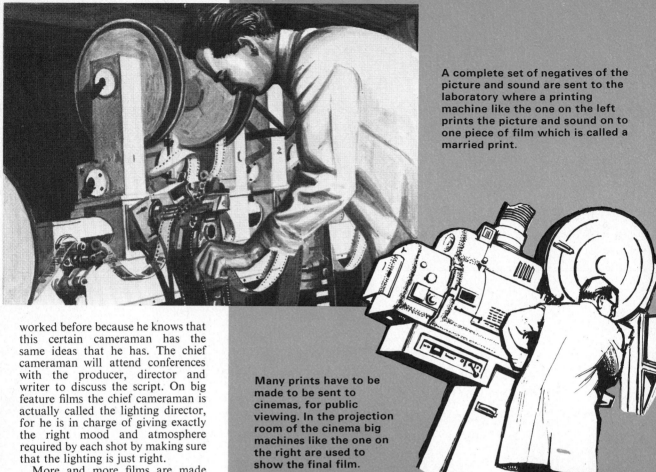

A complete set of negatives of the picture and sound are sent to the laboratory where a printing machine like the one on the left prints the picture and sound on to one piece of film which is called a married print.

Many prints have to be made to be sent to cinemas, for public viewing. In the projection room of the cinema big machines like the one on the right are used to show the final film.

worked before because he knows that this certain cameraman has the same ideas that he has. The chief cameraman will attend conferences with the producer, director and writer to discuss the script. On big feature films the chief cameraman is actually called the lighting director, for he is in charge of giving exactly the right mood and atmosphere required by each shot by making sure that the lighting is just right.

More and more films are made outside studios, 'on location' now. Directors have become much more interested in achieving a realistic effect. Instead of building a mountain of artificial snow inside a studio when a winter snow scene is required, the whole film crew will travel to a snow-covered country to achieve realism. This, of course, makes filming much more complicated. Days are lost because the weather is not right. The sun may be shining brightly in a clear blue sky when a dull overcast day is required for a shot, and vice versa.

A good deal of filming is still done inside studios, though. The lighting director has to arrange the electric lamps for each shot even if the camera angle is only slightly altered. Lighting is so important to the creation of mood and atmosphere that a badly-placed lamp can ruin the whole effect of a scene.

The art director is the next specialist called in on the production team. He designs settings for the scenes which are called sets, and like the lighting, these sets must be entirely in keeping with the mood of the scene, with the characters story, and period. If the film is set in the last century, for example, every detail has to be in keeping with that time in history. As well as needing an extensive knowledge of how people

lived at different periods of history, and an excellent sense of design, the art director has to know all about the craft of film making. His sets have to be practical as well as realistic looking. There has to be enough room for cameramen to move their cameras around the studio, so a good art director has to meet these practical requirements of the cameraman as well as design authentic, beautiful sets.

Before the script is finished, the producer and director will have given considerable thought to the casting of actors and actresses for a film. Sometimes, the producer may have had to promise a film company that he will hire a certain star to act in the film because this will ensure the success of the film. If the producer and director have a reputation for making films that are always great 'box office hits' the film company will allow them much more freedom in their choice of actors and the way in which they go about making the film.

Once all these members of the team have been selected there are still other important people to be hired. The sound supervisor is one of them. He is responsible for everything you hear on the screen.

Dialogue, sound effects and music. On the set the sound is recorded by the same electric motor as the picture camera. This ensures that the sound and picture will be synchronised, that is, they fit together exactly. If they do not, then the words which an actor has to speak may be heard before he has actually opened his mouth!

The director has a number of assistants to help him. The first assistant director makes detailed lists of all the scenes that will take place in the film. If three scenes, for example, require the same setting, they will all be filmed at the same time, even though they appear in different parts of the film. His work of arranging the scenes in the order in which they will be filmed is called breaking down a script. From this, a timetable of the work to be done, called a shooting schedule can be worked out. The assistant director will also be responsible for organising the photographing or shooting of scenes both inside the studio, and outside on location.

Because scenes in films are not actually shot in proper sequence order, someone has to make sure that everything looks the same from one

One of the best character actors in comedy films is Sid James, seen here having his false beard 'adjusted' by a make-up artist before shooting a scene for the film 'Carry on Henry'. King Henry of course, is played by Sid James.

scene to the next, even though three weeks may have elapsed since the preceding scene was shot.

For example, the third scene of the film may be shot at the very beginning of filming and the first scene, which has the same setting, may not be filmed until three weeks later. This means that the set has to look exactly the same and the actors and actresses have to look exactly the same in both scenes.

The person who has to make sure that this happens is the continuity girl. She records a full description of each shot with every minute detail of what props are used, where the set is, how the actors are dressed and so on. Each scene is numbered so that when the next scene is shot she can refer to her list and check the set.

A vitally important member of the production team is the editor. He is responsible for piecing the film together. If a scene has not been shot as well as it should have been and it is too late to re-shoot it, he has to improve it by cutting out pieces. This often happens when a dramatic part of the story is not fast-moving or exciting enough. By cutting out a few feet of film at carefully planned places, the editor can make that scene much more dramatic and achieve the effect which the director wants. He also has to cut and join the filmed dialogue and sound to match the picture.

Once all the basic groundwork is completed, the actual shooting of the film can be started. The evening before the film goes 'on the floor' for the first filming to be done, a sheet of instructions is sent out to everyone involved. This call sheet shows the time that the shooting will begin, which scenes will be shot, and which actors will be needed on the set.

Perhaps the call is for 9 am on the set and this means that everything has to be completely ready for shooting at exactly that time.

That does not mean that everyone starts turning up at the studio at 9 am. It means that many members of the team will have to arrive at 7 am or earlier to prepare the set. Carpenters and electricians see to their work, cameramen have to make sure that their cameras are in perfect working condition and that there is enough film for a day's shooting, the sound men have to make sure that their equipment is working correctly, and actors may have to arrive many hours before filming starts to get made up.

At exactly 9 am the director rehearses the scene with the actors and actresses. Only when he is completely satisfied that everything is ready for a 'take' will the cameras begin to roll.

The sound recordist makes sure that the microphones are picking up the actors' voices clearly, the cameramen look through their lenses to make sure that the lighting is right, the make-up artist quickly touches up an actress's eye make-up, while the hair stylist puts her hair in place.

'Stand by for a take', the assistant director shouts. And the great moment has come for photography to commence. The cameras start to run, the sound recordist cries 'Camera running' and the camera operator says 'Speed up'. 'Mark it', shouts the assistant director, and a board with a number of the scene is held in front of the cameras so that the editor will know where the shot is to go when the film is finished.

The director gives the signal for action and the scene is acted out in front of the rolling cameras just as it has been rehearsed. If the take is not exactly to the director's liking, there will be another, and yet another, until he is completely satisfied.

At the end of the first day's shooting the negative film of pictures and sound is sent to the film laboratory to be developed and printed so that next day they can be projected on to a screen for the director and important members of the team to see. These are called 'rushes' and give the director an opportunity of knowing almost immediately whether certain scenes may need to be shot again.

Once the whole film has been edited the whole soundtrack has to be fitted to the action. This is the time when the film composer is called in to write the music for the film.

When the music 'score' has been recorded all the soundtracks have to be mixed together. They are re-recorded on to a new track so that music, sound effects and dialogue are all on the same track.

After all this is done the complete set of negatives of picture and sound are sent to the laboratory and printed on one piece of film called the married print.

Many prints are made so that they can be sent to the cinemas for public viewing. And once the film has been distributed by the film companies, we have reached the stage that we began with—the moment when the audience sits waiting for the big film to begin.

Arts Quiz

Now you have read the arts section of this book, see how many of the questions you can answer in the quiz below. The answers are at the back of the book.

1 During a period of one hundred years the artists of Holland produced some of the finest works of art the world has known. Which century is popularly known as the Golden Age of Dutch Art?

2 Rembrandt Harmens Van Rijn was born the son of a well-to-do miller at Leyden. In which Dutch city did he become the most important portrait painter?

3 1642 was a year of tragedy for Rembrandt. The wealthy men who had lavished gifts on him no longer wanted his services, and it was also the year in which his wife died. What was her name?

4 The Dutch town of Haarlem produced a portrait painter, who, like Rembrandt had a wonderful gift for capturing human facial expressions. What was his name?

5 Vermeer was the most calm and peaceful of all the Dutch masters. After his death he was forgotten for almost 200 years. From which Dutch town did Vermeer come?

6 Can you name another artist who, like Vermeer, loved to paint the domestic scene and who lived in the same town as Vermeer?

7 Both these artists painted pictures of people going about their daily lives. There is a wonderful feeling of peace in their work. Why is it strange that this peace and tranquility in art seems only to have existed in Holland?

8 After an amazing and adventurous career at sea, Joseph Conrad settled down to become an author and was to be one of England's greatest writers. Can you name the most famous of his novels?

9 Joseph Conrad was not born in England. Where was he born and what was his real name?

10 When Michelangelo was a young student at Lorenzo il Magnifico's School of Sculpture, his face was badly disfigured in a fight with another pupil. After this violent incident he began work on a crowded relief of figures which he was later to value in old age. What was this relief called?

11 Which early sculpture of Michelangelo's, commissioned by a wealthy nobleman for the French chapel at St. Peter's, Rome, made the young artist the most celebrated sculptor in Christendom overnight?

12 Michelangelo's immense knowledge of the anatomy of the human body was unsurpassed in his day. How had he obtained this knowledge?

13 Which of Michelangelo's sculptures is considered his masterpiece and where was it unveiled?

14 The orchestra is always arranged in a certain way. The players are assembled in a large semi-circle on tiers with the conductor in the middle. Can you give two reasons for arranging the orchestra in this way?

15 The stringed instruments form about three-quarters of the orchestra. Do you know, approximately, how many violins are played?

16 When playing the harp a brilliant effect can be achieved when the player sweeps her hand over all the strings. Do you know what this way of playing the harp is called?

17 Name the two types of wind instruments.

18 Which person is responsible for the overall financial arrangements in making a film?

19 A typical camera instruction is "long shot". What does this term mean?

20 What does "tracking" mean?

21 What is the chief cameraman called in feature films?

22 The director of a film has a number of assistants to help him in his work. What is his first assistant responsible for?

23 Because scenes in a film are not actually shot in a natural sequence someone has to make sure that everything looks the same from one scene to the next. What is this person called?

24 When a scene is about to be shot, a board with a number on it is placed in front of the camera. Why is this done?

25 What are "rushes"?

26 What is the name of the little machine which the editor uses for projecting both picture and sound tracks when he is editing?

27 What is meant by the term synchronisation?

28 The evening before a film "goes on the floor" a sheet of instructions is sent out to everyone involved in the film. What is it called?

29 Three soundtracks are used in film-making. What do they each record?

30 What is a married print?

NO CHEATING!

Do not read these answers to the quizzes until you have looked at the questions on pages 24, 48, 80, 104 and 128.

NATURE QUIZ

1. The Japanese rooster. 2. The fresh-water pools of south east Asia. 3. To frighten their enemies away. 4. It makes for the nearest pool. 5. The tube-nosed fruit bat. 6. Taguans, or flying squirrels. 7. It has a long, large nose. 8. The Thunder Bird. 9. The all-powerful sun god, Ra, assumed the form of a hawk. 10. The Phoenix. 11. The albatross. 12. The soul of King Arthur is fabled to have migrated into one of these birds. 13. Seven million years. 14. 200 million years. 15. Cretacious Period. 16. When a species dies out it is usually succeeded by creatures of its kin. This did not happen with dinosaurs. 17. North America. 18. Hoarding nuts and berries in tree holes. 19. Tropical countries. Burma, Siam, Ceylon. 20. Resin. 21. The surface of teak wood does not need to be preserved, it is very durable. 22. Elephants and buffaloes. 23. 120 feet. 24. Wych elm. 25. Central America and parts of South America. 26. Seven years. 27. It means raft in Spanish. The natives of South America used to make their rafts out of balsa wood. 28. They crossed the Pacific on a raft made out of balsa wood. 29. The dead cells inside the wood become filled with air. 30. Fuel and charcoal.

SCIENCE QUIZ

1. Ecology. 2. It was destroyed by a volcanic eruption. Plants and animals have begun to reappear. 3. Ten dustbins. 4. Outer space. 5. The sun. 6. Its corona. 7. The Van Allen Belts. 8. Ch'in. A certain colour. 9. 64 tones; 22 tones. 10. The Sitar. 11. The Indian. 12. A microphone. 13. Electrical currents vibrating at different frequencies. They made notes. 14. A Moog synthesiser. 15. The Industrial Revolution. 16. Oars, sails, rudder. 17. The opening of the Suez canal. 18. A year. 19. Marine turbine and diesel. 20. The invention of the Hovercraft.

21. He flew for a few seconds. 22. Orville and Wilbur Wright. 23. In 1947. 24. Yuri Gagarin. July 20, 1969. 25. William Harvey. 26. One second. 27. Red cells. 28. A thousand gallons. 29. In 1900.

GEOGRAPHY QUIZ

1. The Wall of Death. 2. Fifteen. 3. The maelstrom. 4. The pounds. 5. Spice. 6. Lazarre Picault. 7. Colonel Charles Gordon. He was killed at Khartoum in Africa in 1885. 8. Big Ben. It is on Mahé Island in its capital of Victoria. 9. Tsar Alexander III. Work began on 31st May, 1891. 10. To keep down costs. 11. The State Express. 12. Gold. 13. Edward Hammond Hargraves. 14. They are all gold nuggets. 15. It is the setting for some of the richest gold mines in the world. 16. The heads of their defeated enemies. 17. Bamboo. 18. Rice. 19. James Wilson and Francis Flood. The Flood-Wilson Trans-Africa Motor Cycle Expedition. 20. His banjo. 21. A Tsunami. 22. By radio. 23. Krakatoa. 24. Ecology. 25. One pound. 26. Fifty. 27. Carnivores (*a*). Vegetarians (*b*). 28. The Lepineux chasm. 29. Speleology. 30. A crow.

HISTORY QUIZ

1. It shows a boy riding a bicycle before bicycles were invented. 2. He pushed his feet along the ground. A velocifere. 3. He gave it a steerable front wheel. 4. A Penny Farthing. 5. 1950. The car. 6. The Unknown Warrior. 7. Françoise Simon. In 1916. 8. Belgium, U.S.A., Italy and Britain. Britain. One hundred sacks. 9. Cyrus. 600 B.C. 10. Augustus Caesar. Cursus publicus. 11. Between Columbia and Santiago. 12. April 3, 1860. The telegraph. October 26, 1861. 13. The Huns. 14. The Visigoths. France and Spain. 15. August 4,

A.D. 378. 16. He wanted to keep her birth a secret. 17. Calico Jack. 18. The Governor of Jamaica. 19. He was hanged. 20. The Battle of Trafalgar. Nelson was commander-in-chief of the British ships. 21. Thirty-three. 22. A crescent. 23. Nelson. 24. In 1665. 25. He was four. 26. In 1666. 27. St. Paul's Cathedral. 28. Samuel Pepys. He said that houses should be pulled down to stop the fire spreading. 29. Arthur Wellesley (Duke of Wellington) 30. The Battle of Waterloo, in 1815.

THE ARTS QUIZ

1. Seventeenth century. 2. Amsterdam. 3. Saskia. 4. Franz Hals. 5. Delft. 6. Pieter de Hooch. 7. They lived during Holland's most turbulent and violent time in history. 8. *Lord Jim.* 9. Poland. Konrad Korzeniowski. 10. The Battle of the Centaurs. 11. The First Pieta. 12. He used to creep into mortuaries in order to dissect corpses and find out where the organs of the body were situated. 13. The David Palazzo Vecchio. 14. It enables the players to see the gestures of the conductor and allows the different tones of the instruments to blend well. 15. Forty. 16. Glissando. 17. Woodwind, brass. 18. The producer. 19. A scene photographed from a distance. 20. Pull back camera to give a wider shot. 21. Lighting Director. 22. For breaking down a script, and for organising the photographing of scenes. 23. Continuity Girl. 24. So that the editor will know where the shot is to go when the film has been finished. 25. A rushed print of a day's shooting which is projected on a screen for important members of the production team to view. 26. Moviola. 27. The sound and the pictures are fitted together exactly. 28. A Call sheet. 29. Dialogue, sound effects, music. 30. Complete set of negative pictures and sound printed on to one piece of film.